the NEXT
WAVE

EMPOWERING THE
GENERATION
THAT WILL CHANGE
OUR WORLD

DAVID WRAIGHT

NAVPRESS

OUR GUARANTEE TO YOU

We believe so strongly in the message of our books that we are making this quality guarantee to you. If for any reason you are disappointed with the content of this book, return the title page to us with your name and address and we will refund to you the list price of the book. To help us serve you better, please briefly describe why you were disappointed. Mail your refund request to: NavPress, P.O. Box 35002, Colorado Springs, CO 80935.

The Navigators is an international Christian organization. Our mission is to advance the gospel of Jesus and His kingdom into the nations through spiritual generations of laborers living and discipling among the lost. We see a vital movement of the gospel, fueled by prevailing prayer, flowing freely through relational networks and out into the nations where workers for the kingdom are next door to everywhere.

NavPress is the publishing ministry of The Navigators. The mission of NavPress is to reach, disciple, and equip people to know Christ and make Him known by publishing life-related materials that are biblically rooted and culturally relevant. Our vision is to stimulate spiritual transformation through every product we publish.

Library of Congress Cataloging-in-Publication Data

Wraight, David.
  The next wave : empowering the generation that will change our world / David Wraight.
    p. cm.
  Includes bibliographical references.
  ISBN-13: 978-1-60006-263-6
  ISBN-10: 1-60006-263-6
  1. Missions. 2. Evangelistic work. 3. Church work with young adults. 4. Globalization—Religious aspects—Christianity. I. Title.
  BV2063.W73 2007
  266--dc22

                                                2007028703

Unless otherwise identified, all Scripture quotations in this publication are taken from the HOLY BIBLE: NEW INTERNATIONAL VERSION® (NIV®). Copyright © 1973, 1978, 1984 by International Bible Society. Used by permission of Zondervan Publishing House. All rights reserved. Other versions used include: the *Holy Bible,* New Living Translation (NLT), copyright © 1996, 2004. Used by permission of Tyndale House Publishers, Inc., Carol Stream, Illinois 60188. All rights reserved. Scripture marked (KJV) is from the King James Version.

Produced with the assistance of The Livingstone Corporation (www.LivingstoneCorp.com). Project staff include Neil Wilson, Mary Horner Collins, Larry Taylor, Andy Culbertson, Joel Bartlett, Linda Taylor, and Will Reaves.

Printed in the United States of America
1 2 3 4 5 6 7 8 / 11 10 09 08 07

FOR A FREE CATALOG OF NAVPRESS BOOKS & BIBLE STUDIES,
CALL 1-800-366-7788 (USA) OR 1-800-839-4769 (CANADA).

What Christian Leaders are Saying about *The Next Wave*

This book lives up to the Youth for Christ slogan—"Geared to the times; anchored to the Rock." These accounts of what young people are doing to share Christ around the world make me think of those early days of YFC when we seemed to be living in a constant miracle. Those days are returning! The old principle of "teens winning teens" still works. I recommend this book to every Christian teen, youth leader, YFC worker, and pastor.

Warren Wiersbe
Pastor and Author

The distinctive of this book is that it gives us a genuinely global perspective on young people, youth movements, and the role they play in revolutionizing faith, politics, and society. Written by a youth ministry veteran, it is a clarion call for established leaders to hand the baton to young people in the belief that they will advance the cause of Christ in our time. Westernized youth ministers ought to read this just for the sheer inspirational value gained from what young people are doing in the two-thirds world.

Alan Hirsch
Missional activist and author of
The Forgotten Ways and *The Shaping of Things To Come* (with Mike Frost).
He is also the founding director of Forge Mission Training Network.

"There is still the youngest," Jesse answered, *"but he is tending the sheep."* Samuel said, *"Send for him . . . "* So began the world-shaking journey to spiritual leadership of David, the young man from Bethlehem. Just as Samuel lent the weight of his authority as a prophet to commission and anoint this young leader, David Wraight urges us with passion, spiritual wisdom, and good, practical suggestions to celebrate, empower, and release the wonderful energy of a whole new generation of young people around the globe. The potential is enormous; the price of failure will be devastating. I urge you to read this book!

Mike Treneer
International President
The Navigators

As a surfer I am all for catching the next wave! However, Dave Wraight taps into something far more precious than my next surfing fix. The Next Wave of youth mission is something Dave is passionate about. After decades of youth work, he has the credibility on many levels to speak on these issues. My heart was pounding as I read the key content and the real-life stories. As a "silver surfer" (aged over forty-five!) I need to be challenged about the emerging trends in youth mission, and Dave has done this exceptionally. After reading his work, I feel I am better prepared to catch "the Next Wave"!

Brett Davis
Founder and International Director of
Christian Surfers International

Do you wonder where the world is headed? Wherever that is, young people are leading the way, either to the dark of genocide, terrorism, and nihilism, or to the light of the love of God in Jesus Christ. In this book, David Wraight points the way for the church to grasp the latter goal. His vision is the guiding light of Youth for Christ's strategies in the one hundred nations where YFC operates.

How can you make a lasting difference in the world? Enlist, empower, and support young people. Read this book. It will tell you how.

Sam Wolgemuth
Chair of the Board
Youth for Christ, International

In the 1990s, I witnessed what the devil can do if we give him a chance to influence youth. War, massacres, and genocide in Rwanda are eloquent illustrations of what I am saying. More than one million people perished. A decade later, I am thrilled to see young people with the love of Christ committed to building a new Rwanda with hope and purpose. In *The Next Wave,* David Wraight unveils the formula to change the world either for better or for worse. We have tried this formula in Rwanda and it works. If you want to know that formula, you have the right tool in your hand. Read on.

Jean Baptiste Mugarura
President, Youth for Christ, Rwanda

To the millions of godly, sacrificial, creative, and faithful young people of the world who are sold out to Jesus and are poised to take this world by storm for the sake of the gospel of Jesus Christ and the kingdom of God;

To my much-loved family—my wife, Jenny, and my three children, Belinda, Tracey, and Michael—who throughout my ministry life have believed in me and loved and supported me through good times and bad;

And to my YFC colleagues across the world, whose dedication and servant leadership is an inspiration to me and the young people they so faithfully serve.

CONTENTS

ACKNOWLEDGMENTS

This book is a product of a lifetime journey with young people, and as such I need to acknowledge the many young people who have challenged, inspired, surprised, and amazed me with their creativity, love for others, loyalty, and care for me and my family. They have contributed much to who I am today, and they need to be acknowledged for the part they have played in shaping my life and ministry.

Others also need to be acknowledged for shaping my life and providing me with a solid foundation for an adventurous life of mission and ministry:

Malcolm and Val Wraight—my father and mother—who provided me with a model of unswerving dedication to Jesus, and the invaluable example of a marriage and family built on the principles of *agape* love. They applauded and supported us when Jenny and I first ventured into mission, and continue to this day to provide the encouragement and affirmation we need to follow our calling to reach and serve the young people of the world.

Betty and Kevin Izzard—my "in-laws"—who have showered generosity and love on us, and who have been there for us when we most needed someone to sustain and encourage us. Their advocacy, support, and companionship continually strengthen us on this journey of mission.

Will Cavill—my first mentor—who simply put his arm around a disillusioned teenager and told him that he believed in him and was praying for him every day.

Gordon Blowers, who became our mentor and champion when, as a young couple, we decided to leave our careers to serve Jesus, caring for abused and neglected young people at an Aboriginal community at the edge of the desert in Western Australia.

The leaders of a small church in the southeastern suburbs of Melbourne, who were willing to support me as a young pastor, allowing me to follow a dream of empowering young people to build a radical youth community that effectively reached some of the most marginalized and damaged youth in our city.

The Youth for Christ leaders and global family, who provided me with the opportunity to explore a vision and follow a call, and who continue today to resolutely guard the freedom of young leaders all over the world to develop and implement unique, creative, cutting-edge youth ministry in their indigenous context.

Jean Baptiste Mugarura—my dear brother in Christ—who gently led Jenny and me through the horror of the Rwandan genocide and who has taught us so much about redemption, grace, forgiveness, and love.

My wife, Jenny, for her unending love and support and partnership in this exciting and challenging life that God has called us to.

My children—Belinda, Tracey, and Michael—for believing in their mum and dad, and allowing and supporting them to pursue their calling, with all the upheaval, separation, and sacrifice that comes with a youth ministry life.

My ministry partners at NavPress, and my editor, Neil Wilson, who were prepared to step up and do all that was required to get this book published in a short time frame.

And finally, I wish to acknowledge my Lord and Savior Jesus Christ, who loves me and all the people of this world with an unimaginable love, and who calls us to "make disciples of all nations" by living as His authentic followers in a world that is poised for the *next wave of mission*.

INTRODUCTION

Out beyond the swell bobs a group of surfers, watching, waiting. They sit rising and falling over the swells, listening to the roar of the waves, eyeing the next set of bigger waves. Eagerly they turn beachward and paddle furiously as they are lifted, pushed, then plummet down the towering face of moving water that rises behind and then above them. Riding a great tube, they are flushed out into the channel only to paddle out again.

Time slows. Sometimes you choose to wait for the best wave peaking above the rest. Sometimes you simply decide, *the next wave.* A series of them pulse beneath your board, growing in intensity until you realize, if you don't decide, you won't ride. The waiting is over; actions take over. Your board skims over the water, joining the wave. The move from the paddling position to the standing position is tricky with the board pointed downward and rapidly picking up speed. The power of surf and the pull of gravity surge through your body—overwhelming your senses. This is one of those unforgettable snap-shot moments when the heavens and earth roar the glory of God.

Those life-changing moments can prepare you to recognize other circumstances that bear down on you with a choice: *if you don't decide, you won't ride.* The next wave isn't always made of energy and seawater. God has even more amazing ways to display His glory and power.

I spent much of my youth at the beach. Australia has some of the best surf beaches in the world, and a large majority of Australian young people know how to "ride the waves." I loved the surf, and throughout my childhood and teenage years I spent hours floating around at the back of "the break," waiting for the "perfect" wave. From an early age I would go surfing with anything that I could find that provided me with enough buoyancy to catch a wave—pieces of foam, tire inner tubes, inflatable mattresses—eventually settling on boogie boards and borrowed Malibus.[1]

Surfing is a watching and waiting game. You scan the tide charts and weather pages of the newspaper—or swell forecasts on Internet sites—looking for a convergence of all the right factors that will provide the best conditions for good waves: offshore breeze, large swell, right tide, little chop. On very rare occasions, all the variables come together in the right balance and at the right time. You know that because of this confluence of wind, tide, ocean swell, and weather, there are going to be some huge, airbrushed waves to ride. Everything else in your life is put on hold—job, school, home-life—and the only thing that matters is getting to your favorite spot to ride the waves.

Once you get into the water, you sit on your board for hours scanning the horizon, watching the swells of the ocean, trying to pick the best wave to ride. You can see the swells coming one after another, and you are constantly trying to assess which is the biggest and best-formed swell to ride into the shore. Every now and then you encounter a swell that is two or three times bigger than the rest. You see this "freak wave" coming way out back behind the other swells. You get ready for the "ride of your life," paddling furiously, trying to position yourself in just the right place to catch the wave. But as the swell speeds toward you, getting bigger and bigger, your excitement becomes tinged with fear. *Look at the size of that thing. What if I get dumped by this wave? . . . Man, it's going to pound me into the ocean floor!*

But this is what you have been waiting for all week, or maybe all year, or maybe even all your life. All the conditions and variables have converged at this moment in time to produce the "perfect" wave. Before you know it, it is upon you and you are sliding down the face of a monster. All of your conditioning, physical preparation, and surfing experience are applied at this moment. It is a ride you will never forget. You ride that wave as far as you can, right into the shore, squeezing every bit of joy and fulfillment you can out of that one perfect wave.

The Next Wave is a book about preparing ourselves on all fronts for the "next wave" of mission. It is about reading the signs, trends, and cultural, social, and spiritual shifts that are converging around the world and in the church that tell us that this wave of mission is coming. It is about preparing, empowering, and releasing a generation of young people into mission and ministry throughout the world, as well as the associated challenge before us to serve, nurture, encourage, and resource these young people. And it is about how we, no matter what our age, life situation, available resources, and/or mission experience, can be involved in this tsunami of global mission that has the potential to generate the greatest advance of God's kingdom this world has ever seen.

As globalization and modern technology continue to shrink our world, we are presented with a new landscape that contains amazing possibilities for communicating the love, grace, forgiveness, and hope of the gospel. People are connecting worldwide as never before in the history of humankind—particularly young people—overcoming cultural, geographical, language, and ethnic barriers with ease. Long-standing obstacles are being swept away by the overwhelming tide of information and communication.

However, as we enter this new age of contact and connection, paradoxically people seem to have lost the "art of relationship." Our world is experiencing a global pandemic of loneliness, isolation, and conflict. The foundations of relationship—honesty, trust, faithfulness, loyalty, unconditional love—are in short supply. People are constructing vast virtual realities that turn out to be strangely incapable of meeting the needs that fuel the building effort. Many are searching. They are searching for the truth, they are searching for love, they are searching for relationship, they are searching for meaning and purpose, they are searching for security—they are searching for Jesus. Our world is ready for the next wave of mission, and young people throughout the world are strategically placed to respond to God's call to reach this world with the love and salvation of Jesus Christ.

When young people are given the freedom to lead, abundant fruit is produced. Their simple faith in God constantly generates courageous and creative initiatives, and their connectedness to the cutting edge of societal change allows them to be relevant and effective in their mission strategies. They have boundless energy and an absolute belief in the God of the impossible.

Biblical and church history is replete with examples of faithful, energetic, and courageous young people being used by God to bring about change, renewal, and blessing. Young people have been the instigators of every major mission movement over the past two hundred years, and once again they are at the forefront of a new wave of mission that is gaining momentum across the world. We can try to let this wave pass and miss what God is doing, or we can become part of *the next wave.*

Empowering a generation of globally connected young people to engage in mission is one of the most strategic things the church can do to advance the kingdom of God. However, making the most of this global mission opportunity doesn't only involve freeing an emerging generation to reach the world for Christ. Biblical stewardship responsibilities, the personal call of our God to grow His kingdom on this earth, and the biblical imperatives to support and nurture younger Christians, demand that *all* believers get involved.

Each of us has a key role to play in supporting and serving an emerging generation of world-changing followers of Jesus. To be able to achieve their full potential, they need us to stand with them, cheering them on, providing affirmation and solidarity. Christians of all ages need to pray for them, mentor them, encourage them, equip them, protect them, and allow them to lead. And along with supporting and serving this generation at the cutting edge of mission, believers also need to be ready to receive a massive harvest of new believers. This will require those of us in the church today to live as revolutionary, authentic, disciple-making followers of Jesus, providing welcoming and supportive transformational communities of mature believers—believers who can say as Paul did, "Follow my example, as I follow the example of Christ."

NOTES
1. A Malibu is a ten- to fourteen-foot-long surfboard.

CHAPTER ONE

THE POTENTIAL OF
YOUNG PEOPLE TO
CHANGE THE WORLD

In 1993, at the age of twenty-eight, Jean Baptiste Mugarura was going places. He had a diploma in law, was fluent in five languages, and had a good job in the National Bank of Rwanda. But God had different plans for Jean Baptiste beyond his career in international banking. God started to work on Jean Baptiste's heart, giving him a vision for reaching the young people of his nation.

Jean Baptiste heard about the ministry of Youth for Christ from the YFC International president, Gerry Gallimore, whom he had met in Singapore when Jean Baptiste attended the Advanced Leadership Training at Haggai Institute. Gerry Gallimore came to speak during one of the evening devotions. Later, Jean Baptiste contacted him to explore the possibilities of establishing a YFC ministry in Rwanda.

By the time the YFC Africa Area Director, Don Osman, visited Jean Baptiste and his "ministry committee" in January 1994, they had made significant progress. They had developed an extensive outreach and support program to the street kids of

Kigali and had conducted numerous youth outreach programs and events in many parts of the country. They were establishing strong partnerships with local churches. They had sixty volunteers involved in various levels of the ministry, and Jean Baptiste was in the process of withdrawing from his position at the bank to take on a full-time role with YFC. Don was much encouraged by what he saw and returned to the area office with a plan to officially "charter" the ministry of Jean Baptiste and his YFC team. However, it was only a few months after Don's visit that the ongoing rebel war and the simmering Rwandan civil strife boiled over into furious genocide and massacres.

A jaded and then shocked world looked on in silence as over one million people were slaughtered in only one hundred days, and most were killed with machetes and clubs! The brutality and extent of this genocide is impossible to comprehend and can only really be understood by those who lived through it.

The genocide was perpetrated by the Rwandan government. At the time there were only three identifiable tribes in Rwanda: the Hutu, the Tutsi, and the Twa. The Hutu were the ruling tribe since independence in 1962. The Tutsi, being a repressed minority, were constantly rebelling against the rule of the Hutu. In an attempt to control the Tutsi dissidents, the government mobilized a Hutu youth militia they called the *Interahamwe*[1] in towns and communities across Rwanda.

The interesting thing about Rwanda is that all the people of Rwanda are from one ethnic group, speaking the same language, inhabiting the same areas, intermarrying, and following the same traditions. It was the Belgian colonists who perpetuated and exaggerated the intra-tribal divisions, eventually producing identity cards in 1932 that arbitrarily classified people as either Hutu or Tutsi. From that time on, the Belgian rulers played one tribe against the other, intensifying the racial divide and creating an environment of hatred and ethnic discrimination. Rounds of violence between Hutu and Tutsi kept social conditions in continuous turmoil not only in Rwanda but also in Burundi. The Rwandan genocide was a particularly shameful and gruesome chapter in a long story of unrest and injustice.

At the time of the genocide, the main radio station in Rwanda was controlled by the radical Hutu government and the militia. The majority of the people in the nation listened constantly to this station for news, music, entertainment, and information. Hence, a large percentage of the population of Rwanda could be mobilized in a very short time. On the first day of the genocide a mandate was issued over the radio to the militia leaders and all faithful Hutu to rid Rwanda of every Tutsi. The literal instructions were "exterminate the *Inyenzi*" (cockroaches). The genocidal frenzy erupted in Kigali and swept across the nation.

The killing was not limited to the Tutsi. Israel Havugimana—a prominent African Christian leader and evangelist—had mentored Jean Baptiste for many years. On the first day of the genocide this man and two of his children were slaughtered in their home. Both Jean Baptiste and Israel came from the Hutu tribe, yet they were prime targets because, leading up to the genocide, they had been advocating for peace, tolerance, and reconciliation between the Tutsi and Hutu.

Prior to the genocide, the Hutu militia had been provided with death lists identifying in order of importance all those to be "exterminated." Many Christian leaders were singled out because of their stand for justice, reconciliation, and peace.

After the murder of Israel Havugimana, Jean Baptiste knew that he was most likely next in line on the death list. He had already fled Kigali and was moving from town to town across the nation in an attempt to escape the militia death squads.

Choosing who should be killed was a subjective and cruel roulette. Jean Baptiste shared with me a story about a friend of his who was trying to escape Rwanda. He had to pass through a militia roadblock on his way out of the nation. At the roadblock the militia guards looked at his identity card and saw that he was Hutu. Those who had Tutsi identity cards were killed immediately, but Hutu were generally allowed to pass. However, the militia at this particular roadblock had devised another test to determine the veracity of those with Hutu identity cards. They decided to confirm the stereotype that Tutsi were a taller people than the Hutu. So they drew a line on a power pole, and everyone who passed though the roadblock was made to stand up against the pole. One of the militia then hacked off with a machete any part of the person's body that was above the line.

Unfortunately, Jean Baptiste's friend was a tall man and most of his head protruded above the line on the pole. As the militia prepared to cut off his head, he pointed across to one of the people standing nearby and asked who he was. The militia leader identified him as one of the roadblock guards. Seeing that this guard was very tall, Jean Baptiste's friend suggested to the militia that they make the guard stand up against the pole. Amazingly, the militia leader agreed, and when the guard was measured on the pole, his whole head was above the line. Laughing and joking with his fellow guards, the militia leader sent Jean Baptiste's friend on his way. Through a spur-of-the-moment ploy and a whimsical response of a militia leader, this man was able to escape a brutal death.

Throughout the hundred days of slaughter, Jean Baptiste continued to move from town to town, trying to keep ahead of the militia who were intent on killing him. On a number of occasions he was captured by the militia and was literally seconds from being killed, but in each case God miraculously intervened and saved him. By the end of the hundred days Jean Baptiste's fiancée, nearly all his sixty volunteer staff, the YFC committee chairman, and most of the YFC committee members and their families had been murdered. The cost was immeasurable; the grief overwhelming.

A booklet published by the Kigali Memorial Center[2] graphically describes the genocide:

In 100 days more than 1,000,000 people were murdered.

But the genocidaires did not kill a million people. They killed one, then another, then another . . . . day after day, hour after hour, minute by minute. Every minute of the day, someone, somewhere was being murdered, screaming for mercy.

Receiving none.

And the killing went on and on and on . . .

10,000 each day,

400 each hour,

7 each minute.

The genocide resulted in the deaths of over a million people.

But death was not the only outcome.

Tens of thousands of people had been tortured, mutilated and raped; tens of thousands more suffered machete cuts, bullet wounds, infection and starvation.

There was rampant lawlessness, looting and chaos. The infrastructure had been destroyed, the ability to govern dismantled. Homes had been demolished, belongings stolen.

There were over 300,000 orphans and over 85,000 children who were heads of their household, with younger siblings and/or relatives.

There were thousands of widows. Many had been victims of rape and sexual abuse or had seen their own children murdered.

Many families had been totally wiped out, with no one to remember or document their deaths.

The streets were littered with corpses. Dogs were eating the rotting flesh of their owners.

The country smelled of the stench of death.

The genocidaires had been more successful in their evil aims than anyone would have dared to believe.

Rwanda was dead.

How could a million people be killed in such a brutal way and in such a short period of time? The tragic fact is that this horrific genocide was achieved by mobilizing the youth of Rwanda. It was teenagers and young adults who carried out most of the slaughter. By empowering young people and harnessing all of their energy, creativity, naiveté, and unswerving commitment to a cause, the Hutu leaders were able to orchestrate one of the most brutal and horrific acts of ethnic cleansing the world has ever experienced. Children as young as nine and ten years old were given guns and instructed to use them against those the militia targeted for death. How could the reality of evil not be seen in the acts of those who caused, in Jesus' words, "the little ones to stumble" in such unspeakable ways?

A Memorial to Unbridled Evil

In 2005 my wife, Jenny, and I visited Rwanda to participate in a series of events celebrating ten years of ministry since the re-establishment of Youth for Christ in the nation. While we were in Rwanda, Jean Baptiste drove us out to a genocide memorial site. It was at this memorial site that we were confronted with the full horrors of the genocide.

The memorial consists of a church compound in which over five thousand people were slaughtered. When the militia started rounding up the people they had selected to be killed, many ran to the church, thinking they would be safe in a "house of God." Between two and three hundred people squeezed into the small church building that would normally hold around one hundred worshippers. Most were women and children. When the militia found the people in the church, they certainly weren't daunted by the fact it was a house of God. They immediately started throwing grenades into the building through the open windows. After the grenades had done their work, they entered the church and slaughtered any left alive with machetes. They then proceeded to kill the remaining five thousand people they had gathered in the open area surrounding the church.

After the slaughter, the few local people left alive could not bring themselves to clean up the carnage. They just left the decomposing bodies where they lay. For several years the church was left untouched, until the government finally sent in a team of people to clean up the site. However, instead of burying the bodies, which were now bleached bones, the government leaders decided that they would make this church a genocide memorial. They gathered together the remains of those killed in the church compound, placing them in two small buildings near the church. They then took most of the skulls from the remains and stacked them on shelves at the back of the church building. However, apart from putting shelves in the back of the church to hold the skulls, they left the interior of the building as they found it.

When Jenny and I entered the church, we were confronted with shelf upon shelf stacked from floor to ceiling with skulls marred by obvious cracks and holes where they had been smashed with machetes. The stark evidence of demonic brutality was everywhere. As we moved farther into the church we had to walk on the benches (backless pews) because the bones, clothes, and remains of those killed in the church completely covered the floor between the benches, up to the level of the seats. There were small shoes of children on the benches, a child's skull on the altar at the front of the church, and clothes, bones, and personal items completely covering the floor. We then walked somberly from the church to the two small buildings nearby. Two huge piles of the remains of the people who were killed were stacked up in each building. This encounter with such raw, unbridled evil shook me to the core of my being.

Since visiting this memorial I have reflected much on the experience. My view of life's purpose has been altered. One of the results of my desire not to ignore or forget what I saw in Rwanda is that I have become even more committed to countering the evil and injustice of Satan's rule by following the mandate of Jesus to establish His kingdom on this earth. And I'm discovering that others share my vision around the world. It isn't a new vision, but one that echoes down through history.

Booth's Vision

William Booth, the founder of the Salvation Army, when talking about his passion to reach the lost with the gospel of Jesus Christ, often shared the vision that God had given to him early in his ministry years. In his vision Booth saw dark clouds and lightning hovering over a billowing, stormy ocean filled with thousands of people screaming for help, struggling for safety. A huge rock rose up out of the ocean into the clouds. Around the rock stretched a platform filled with people. A few of them tried to help the drowning ones, using ropes, ladders, and boats. But most people on the platform went about their business, oblivious to those in the sea—even their drowning friends. Although they heard the cries, the platform people spent their time tending their flower gardens, raising their families, and begging God for assurance that they would one day reach security at the top of the mountain.

When sharing this vision, William Booth would often say, "I wish I could take each of my workers and, for just five minutes, dangle them over the fires of hell, to give them added incentive to pursue the lost, to give them a taste of what the people they are trying to reach are going to." Visiting the memorial site in Rwanda was my "taste of hell," and it has spurred me on to be even more diligent and committed to reaching this world with the love of Jesus.

A Miracle of God's Grace

You might expect that it would be impossible for a nation to recover from such brutality and evil. However, when you visit Rwanda today, you are confronted with an absolute miracle of God's grace and love. Just as Satan used the youth of a nation to destroy, murder, and pillage, so God is now using the youth of Rwanda to rebuild the nation and to bring about enormous change for good.

After the genocide, Jean Baptiste escaped Rwanda—a battered and haunted survivor. He was cared for and counseled for six months by the YFC Africa Area staff. But after those months of healing and restoration, he returned to Rwanda to once again take up the task God had assigned him. He spent the first few years simply traveling back and forth across the nation, preaching reconciliation and forgiveness. Then he started to rebuild the YFC ministry.

Jean Baptiste set about mobilizing a huge force of young people to reach his nation with a message of salvation, forgiveness, and grace. By the end of 2005, only ten years after the genocide—through empowering young leaders and working in partnership with local churches, pastors, and denominational leaders—450,000 young people had been reached, with over 75,000 of these young people committing their lives to Christ. Nearly all of these new Christians are now involved in local churches and ongoing discipleship programs.

Rwanda is now a nation being rebuilt by young people who are sold out to Jesus and who, in the face of unbelievable suffering, evil, and destruction, are living out the values of God's kingdom—love, grace, forgiveness, purity, self-sacrifice, and servanthood. The tribal hatred that was the driving force behind the genocide has been overcome by forgiveness and lasting reconciliation. It is no longer appropriate to ask Rwandans whether they are Hutu or Tutsi, because this has become illegal. They are one people now, and if asked what tribe they are from, they will simply reply that they are Rwandan.

Jenny and I had the privilege of spending ten days with several hundred young leaders while we were in Rwanda. All of them had lost family or friends to the genocide. All of them had seen and experienced brutality, murder, and violence to a degree that staggers belief. Yet, we were overwhelmed by the grace, generosity, sacrificial love, forgiving nature, passion for the lost, and overall godliness of these young people. God had wrought a miracle of redemption and grace in their lives.

Redemption in Rwanda

Visit Rwanda today and you will hear story after story of the redemption, grace, forgiveness, and reconciliation that is sweeping across the nation. In their own way these accounts are as stunning as the violence that set the stage for God's amazing work. During the genocide a militia leader led a band of *Interahamwe* on a killing rampage through a village. A woman who lived in this village witnessed the murder of her husband and all her children at the hand of this teenager and his followers. However, not long after this incident, this militia leader himself suffered a tragic loss: his whole family—mother, father, and all his brothers and sisters—were murdered.

After the genocide, this young man was identified as one of the perpetrators of the slaughter in his village. He was convicted by a local community court and sent to prison. The prisons of Rwanda were full to capacity, and there were simply not enough resources available to provide food and care for all the inmates. The only way that prisoners could survive in the prison system was if family members provided them with food and the basic necessities of life. Because this young militia leader's family had all been killed, he had no one to care for him and he was in a desperate state.

News soon got around the village about this man's plight. When the woman whose family this young man had murdered heard about his situation, she responded in uncharacteristic fashion. She neither rejoiced in his suffering nor saw his condition as a way to satisfy a desire for vengeance. Being a believer in Christ, she knew that God's Word required that she love this murderer of her family with the "unconditional" love of Jesus. She knew that she needed to forgive and seek reconciliation. And so in obedience to her Lord, she visited this young man in prison. She told him she forgave him. She explained that she knew he had lost all of his family and needed a family to bring him food. She said that they needed each other: he needed a family to care for him, and she needed a family to care for. And so she adopted this young man as her own son, and she loved him as only a mother can love a son. What this godly woman gave to this young man was far more than the food he needed for physical survival. Through the unconditional love and forgiveness of Jesus, she provided him with the spiritual and emotional healing he desperately needed to restore his tortured soul.

A Purpose-Driven Nation

During the ten-year celebration festival we attended, a number of the Rwandan government ministers were invited to visit the YFC training center to participate in some of the events. One of these ministers who accepted the invitation was the Minister

THE POTENTIAL OF YOUNG PEOPLE

for Youth, Sport, and Culture. He was given the opportunity to speak to a group of two hundred young people who were involved in a leadership training program. As this man stood before these young leaders, he noticed some posters that hung on the walls that described the characteristics of Christian young leaders listed under four headings—prowess in spiritual warfare, boldness in evangelism, passion in social involvement, and godliness in leadership. We had been using the characteristics on these posters as the framework for our teaching.

The minister folded up his prepared speech and put it aside. He then declared that he was a Christian and that these biblical principles on the posters were the principles that were going to be used as the foundation for rebuilding Rwanda. He pointed at the young leaders and said that they, and other Christian young people like them, were the people who would lead their nation into the future.

Later that day we were in the lobby of a hotel with Jean Baptiste. He saw a woman in the lobby and recognized her as another of the Rwandan government ministers. He immediately walked up to her and identified himself. She acknowledged that she knew who he was. Jean Baptiste told her that he had been praying for her. She asked what he had been specifically praying for. He replied: "I have been praying that you would find a personal relationship with Jesus." She replied: "That prayer has already been answered. I gave my life to Jesus last week."

Rwanda has now become a shining beacon of light in one of the darkest regions in Africa. In a little over ten years Rwanda has transitioned from being a nation that experienced one of the greatest evils ever visited upon humanity to a nation that is being rebuilt on the principles of God's Word.

The Power of Young People to Change Our World

When young people are mobilized in large numbers, they have an enormous synergistic capacity to bring about change in the world. Throughout history there have been a number of political leaders who have recognized this collective world-changing potential of youth and have used the youth of their nation to bring about eras of change that have significantly impacted the world. Unfortunately, in nearly every instance where young people have been mobilized to bring about national or global change, it has been under the leadership of despots and dictators whose agendas of control, violence, and repression have caused enormous pain and suffering.

Adolf Hitler was well aware of the power of youth. During a speech at the Reichsparteitag in 1935, Hitler declared, "He alone who owns the youth gains the future." By mobilizing the youth of Germany through a movement called "Hitler Youth," Hitler was able to seize control of Germany, drive his agenda of world domination and genocide, and usher in World War II, which ultimately resulted in the deaths of sixty-two million people.[3]

Hitler capitalized on the idealism, loyalty, and creativity of youth. Using training camps and weekly club meetings, he captivated the hearts and minds of the young people of Germany, providing them with a collective vision that focused all of their youthful energy in world-changing action. Speaking of his youth mobilization program Hitler stated, "My program for educating youth is hard. Weakness must be hammered away. In my castles of the Teutonic Order a youth will grow up before which the world will tremble. I want a brutal, domineering, fearless, cruel youth. Youth must be all that. It must bear pain. There must be nothing weak and gentle about it. The free, splendid beast of prey must once again flash from its eyes. . . . That is how I will eradicate thousands of years of human domestication. . . . That is how I will create the New Order."[4]

Mao Zedong is another political leader who mobilized the youth of his nation, and through this mobilization was able to wrest power from other political leaders and gain control of China. Fighting an attempt to marginalize him, Mao initiated the Cultural Revolution, which circumvented the Communist hierarchy by giving power directly to the Red Guards—groups of young people, often teenagers, who set up their own tribunals of terror and control. Squads of teenage Red Guards would go from house to house looking for potential elements of corruption, using the *Little Red Book*[5] as their doctrinal and behavioral point of reference to assess the acceptability of those they were investigating. The Revolution led to the destruction of much of China's cultural heritage and the imprisonment of a huge number of Chinese intellectuals, as well as creating general economic and social chaos in the country. Millions of people were killed and displaced and many other lives were ruined during this period of youth-driven revolution.[6]

Along with Hitler's Youth and Mao's Red Guards, the story of Rwanda provides us with convincing evidence that empowering young people and allowing them to lead can bring about enormous change in the world, either for good or for evil. The young people of Rwanda were mobilized to destroy a nation; they became instruments in the hands of Satan and perpetrators of horrendous acts of violence and destruction.

But the story of the mobilization of the young people of Rwanda didn't finish at the end of the genocide. The ongoing story of Rwanda is a story of redemption, of God's redeploying the youth of a nation to bring about healing, reconciliation, forgiveness, and love in the face of the seemingly insurmountable obstacles of hate, revenge, and bitterness. It is a story of enormous change for good orchestrated by the young people of a nation; a story that I believe can be replicated in many other nations and regions of the world. Rwanda provides us with hope—that through young, courageous followers of Jesus Christ, the kingdom of God can be established in the darkest strongholds of Satan.

If young people of a nation are able to change the course of history, acting together with a common vision and purpose under the direction of a corrupt and flawed human leader, imagine what changes will be wrought in the world when a global community of young people starts acting together under the direction and leadership of Jesus Christ!

NOTES

1. *Interahamwe* means "those who attack together."

2. The Kigali Memorial Center was opened to mark the tenth anniversary commemoration of the genocide. The center is situated in the district of Gisozi, the site chosen for the mass burial of the 250,000 victims of the genocide in Kigali, the capital city of Rwanda.

3. Wikipedia, "World War II," http://en.wikipedia.org/wiki/World_War_Two

4. The History Place, "Hitler Youth," http://www.historyplace.com/worldwar2/hitleryouth

5. A collection of quotations excerpted from Mao Zedong's speeches and publications.

6. Wikipedia, "Mao Zedong," http://en.wikipedia.org/wiki/Mao_Zedong#Cultural_Revolution

CHAPTER TWO

THE IMPACT OF
YOUNG PEOPLE

I wasn't far into my journey of Christian ministry leadership before I discovered that if you want to be effective in youth ministry, you need to surround yourself with a team of young leaders. So when I was appointed as National Director of Youth for Christ Australia, I was thrilled when God gathered around me a team of vibrant, creative, and talented young people.

The YFC ministry had been through a rigorous period of soul-searching and renewal from which came a new vision: "That *every* young person in Australia has the opportunity to be a follower of Jesus Christ." Of course, the very nature of a vision is that it is way bigger than your capabilities and available resources, and in YFC our resources were very limited and our dreams very big.

As we grappled with this vision to reach the young people of Australia, the most significant challenge confronting us was the implication of the phrase "every young person." If we were to take this vision seriously, how were we going to gain access to *all* the young people of Australia? We explored many possibilities, but eventually came across a unique opportunity. We discovered that enshrined in the legislation of every state and territory in Australia was the provision for Christian Religious Education (CRE) in all secondary schools. There was actually a law in each state and territory that required that secondary school students receive thirty minutes of CRE per week!

God had provided a unique way for us to gain access to nearly every young person in Australia in the age range we were endeavoring to reach. So we set out to find the most effective way to take advantage of this legislative provision. I presented my young team of leaders at YFC with the challenge of developing a mission strategy that would enable us to make the most of the opportunity to conduct CRE programs in secondary schools across the nation.

Young Leaders in Action
One of the exciting things about young people is that they are largely unaffected by organizational or denominational loyalties. Leaders primarily interested in keeping everything unchanged may find this trait nerve-racking. But youthful minds take a unified and creative approach to mission, drawing upon the collective resources of the church to come up with innovative, efficient, and effective mission strategies. So when presented with the strategic challenge of delivering CRE programs in all the secondary schools in Australia, my team of young leaders immediately looked for allies in the vision. They perceived that the only way to achieve this vision was to develop a ministry model that maximized strategic partnerships with other missions and the local church, drawing upon the wide variety of resources, specialties, and giftedness available in God's family in Australia.

They started coming up with brilliant, outrageous, and—from my perspective—completely unworkable ideas. However, one proposal that kept overcoming obstacles and gaining support was an all-day seminar that involved multimedia, film, music, vox-pops,[1] small groups, and simulation games.[2] The genius of this program was that it actually required local church involvement for it to work, as well as providing ample opportunity for partnership with other youth ministries. It also allowed us to approach schools with an offer to amalgamate all of their mandated thirty-minute CRE into a one-day experience for all the students in a particular year level.

The program was called "AusLife," and once it was introduced it took off. The schools loved it, and the churches that partnered with YFC and other youth ministries running the program were overwhelmed with the number of young people they were able to connect with and follow up. And best of all, the young people responded! We found that at the end of a one-day seminar, 10 to 20 percent of the students who participated indicated on a "react card" that they wanted to know more about having a relationship with Jesus Christ. These young people were followed up through further outreach and discipleship programs conducted by the local church.

In the developmental phase of the AusLife program, one young leader on the YFC team stood out as a brilliant and creative strategist with an unshakable and courageous faith. Her name was Glenda. Teammates and observers alike sensed God had uniquely gifted Glenda to lead this ministry, and so I appointed this bold twenty-four-year-old to oversee the whole AusLife program in Australia.

Glenda very quickly recruited a multitalented team of young people to extend and expand the impact of AusLife. This team was soon able to harness all that the latest in technology and multimedia had to offer, and they came up with incredibly creative and relevant programs that greatly increased the popularity and effectiveness of the AusLife program. Glenda brokered numerous strategic partnerships with other youth ministries to enable us to deliver the AusLife program to schools in all the major cities in Australia. AusLife very quickly became one of the key youth outreach ministry strategies in Australia, mobilizing and equipping local churches to collectively pursue the vision to provide every young person in the nation with the opportunity to be a follower of Jesus Christ. The impossible vision was becoming visible reality.

Unfortunately, we soon ran into a major problem. As the program expanded and became more prominent, I was contacted by a number of people who pointed out that by using clips from movies, music videos, and television programs, we were breaking multiple copyright laws. It was obvious that if we didn't change the way we were doing things, we would inevitably end up in a serious legal battle that had the potential to cripple the program, and possibly even jeopardize the financial viability of the whole organization.

I explained the situation to Glenda and suggested we might have to find a way to continue the program without using video clips. Glenda was horrified. She told me in no uncertain terms that the whole program relied on multimedia and music, and that it would be impossible to connect with the students without using film, music, and television clips, which expressed the youth culture and identified the issues that the AusLife program was trying to address.

Glenda said she would find a way around the problem. "After all," she reminded me, "God has given us this program to reach the young people of Australia, . . . He'll provide a way through this."

I countered by reminding her that we were dealing with the law of the land, and we had a biblical mandate to comply with that law. Unless we could address the copyright issue, we had to stop using the videos. Although I encouraged Glenda to continue to explore possible solutions, I started thinking through how we could restructure the program to eliminate the threat.

Glenda started contacting the movie and media distributors to obtain their permission to use the film clips and music videos. It wasn't long before she came back to me, frustrated but not defeated. She shared with me how much the media distributors wanted us to pay for the rights to use their products. Licensing involved huge amounts of money, and because we continually updated and changed the material, it was going to cost us a fortune to comply with the copyright law.

Once again I encouraged Glenda to redesign the program, and once again she refused to even consider this, advocating that using the multimedia material was essential for the Aus-Life program's success. She reiterated that God would provide a way to get past the copyright problem. I continued to explore other alternatives.

A few days later Glenda came to me very excited. She informed me that Coral, one of her team members, had found a way to overcome the copyright problem. We simply had to get the Australian Federal Parliament (the governing body of Australia) to declare Youth for Christ exempt from copyright law for the purpose of their school programs. Since the law was theirs, they could certainly declare us an exception to the rule. Simple! I jokingly asked Glenda to get the Prime

Minister on the phone right away so we could arrange for parliament to declare us exempt. Undaunted, Glenda left my office convinced she had found a way to solve the problem. I worked even more diligently on planning major changes to the AusLife program.

Very soon Glenda was back in my office. She told me that Coral had been able to connect with a prominent lawyer in Canberra,[3] whose job was to write legislation for the government. Although this lawyer wasn't a Christian, he was very interested in what YFC was doing in the schools and he was willing to help. Over the next few weeks I watched in amazement as this lawyer lobbied on our behalf, and the Attorney General of Australia, with the endorsement of the Australian Federal Parliament, declared a copyright exemption for YFC Australia. I joyfully scrapped my alternative plans.

Empowering Young People to Lead

This experience of witnessing Glenda's leadership and the creativity and adaptability of her team taught me a valuable lesson: I realized that to be effective in youth ministry, it isn't enough just to surround ourselves with young leaders so they can "help" us with our mission. Rather, it is essential that we empower young people by allowing them to truly lead. In fact, as I have continued in youth ministry and mission, I have come to realize that empowering young people is not only the key to effective youth mission, but it is the key to effective mission in any context.

Glenda expressed the simple, uncomplicated, and unshakable faith of youth, and the Lord harnessed her youthful naiveté and "never-say-never" attitude to achieve His purposes. Through Glenda's leadership, courage, and confidence in the

God of the impossible, the impossible was achieved. AusLife was salvaged from ineffectiveness, and tens of thousands of young people were reached—and continue to be reached—through this program.

The fact is, when young people are given the freedom to lead, amazing fruit is produced. Their healthy naiveté constantly generates courageous and creative initiatives, and their connectedness to the cutting edge of societal change allows them to be relevant and effective in their mission strategies. They have boundless energy and an unshakable faith in God. Because of these unique attributes, involving young people at the most strategic levels of mission and ministry is essential for the church to remain relevant in a rapidly changing society. Allowing young people to lead will open up the potential for miraculous growth and effectiveness in mission.

Often young people are seen as "future" leaders, as the "next" generation, and, in one sense, they are the "positional" community and church leaders of the future. But we also need to see young people as leaders for "now," and we need to provide opportunities for them to lead today.

Young people have a vital role to play in leading the worldwide Christian community into new arenas of effective, radical, kingdom-building ministry. They are the key to the church being relevant in the world because they are "agents of change," full of hopes and dreams of "what can be" rather than being content with "what is." Living in a world where the pace of change increases every day, we desperately need young people to lead as agents of change in the church and in the broader community, helping us to be relevant and connected and therefore effective in outreach.

This is clearly supported by a review of biblical history, where we find numerous examples of faithful and courageous young people being used by God to bring about change, renewal, and blessing.

Young Leaders in Biblical History
David

A mere teenager, David courageously fought the giant Goliath when experienced, well-trained soldiers and military leaders were afraid to take on this seemingly impossible task.[4] David was sent by his father, Jesse, to take some food to his three brothers who were serving with the Israelite army. The Israelites were camped in the Valley of Elah preparing to fight the Philistines. Every day, for forty days, the Philistine champion Goliath—who stood over nine feet tall—strode out to the battle line and challenged the Israelites to send out one man to fight him, taunting and ridiculing King Saul and his army in the process.

David arrived at the camp just as Goliath was issuing his daily challenge. Astounded at the Israelites' fearful reaction to Goliath's taunts, David started asking the soldiers around him why someone didn't just get out there and deal with this "uncircumcised Philistine." With youthful exuberance he offered to go and fight the giant himself. Can you imagine what those battle-hardened soldiers thought when an inexperienced teenage shepherd boy challenged them about their fear and reluctance to fight Goliath and the Philistine army? David's brothers were furious. Extremely embarrassed by his behavior, they began haranguing him for being such a conceited and naïve young man.

When King Saul was informed of this teenager's bravado, he too pointed out David's naiveté, stating that he was "just a boy" and that he had no idea what he was up against. But Saul had run out of options. No one in his army was prepared to take on Goliath, including Saul himself. And so he sent out a teenager to fight the Philistine champion—without any weapons or armor—obviously expecting him to fail. But David knew that his God was way bigger than this giant; and through the simple and uncomplicated faith of youth he was able to succeed where adults had failed, defeating Goliath with a sling and a stone,[5] and leading the Israelite army to victory. When everyone else saw in Goliath an enemy too strong to defeat, David saw a target too big to miss! The story of David and Goliath is a classic biblical example of how God uses the naiveté, idealism, and unquestioning faith of youth to achieve His purposes.

Josiah

When he was only twenty years old, King Josiah instituted a great reformation in Judah.[6] Due to some misguided and ungodly leadership, the nation of Judah had drifted into a period of idol worship and complete neglect of God and His ways. At the age of eight Josiah was appointed king. As he grew into his leadership role, he began to discover that the religious practices of his people were a long way from what God required of them. In fact, when God's Law was first read to him, Josiah was so distraught that he wept and tore his clothes.[7] Simply applying the values of God's Word and Law to his life and leadership, this young man became an agent of change in his nation. Josiah's youthful passion, absolute commitment to the application of God's truth in his life, and willingness to go against the flow of cultural norms and traditions resulted in leading his nation—at a very young age—into an extended period of obedience and service to God.

Shadrach, Meshach, and Abednego

Shadrach, Meshach, and Abednego—three young men most likely under the age of twenty at the time of their confrontation with the king of Babylon—refused to bow down and worship an image of King Nebuchadnezzar.[8] The king had set up a ninety-foot golden statue of himself in the plain of Dura, and had gathered together all the officials and servants of his kingdom for a time of worship before his image. Shadrach, Meshach, and Abednego were in training to serve in the king's palace, and so they were required to attend the image-worship event. But they were Jews and followers of the one true God. They refused to worship anyone, or anything, except their God. And so when the music played and everyone else bowed before the image, three young men were left standing.

The king was furious. He threatened to throw the three friends into a blazing furnace if they continued to defy his command. Even facing the threat of being burned alive, Shadrach, Meshach, and Abednego remained true to their commitment to God, declaring that their God was more than able to deliver them. But they also acknowledged God's discretionary power over their lives, stating that even if their God chose not to deliver them, they would still worship and follow Him.[9]

So the king had them thrown into the furnace, and to Nebuchadnezzar's amazement, God not only delivered Shadrach, Meshach, and Abednego, but He—or one of His angels—also appeared with them in the flames. We are told that when they came out of the furnace, "the satraps, prefects, governors and royal advisers crowded around them. They saw that the fire had not harmed their bodies, nor was a hair of their heads singed; their robes were not scorched, and there was no smell of fire on them."[10] When Nebuchadnezzar witnessed this miracle, he praised the God of these courageous and faithful young men.

Shadrach, Meshach, and Abednego trusted God implicitly, never doubting His character and care. They also acknowledged God's sovereignty over their lives, and were prepared to die for Him, if that was what He required. Through their faith and testimony to God's character, three young men were able to introduce the king of Babylon to the one true God, and change the spiritual focus of the most powerful nation in the ancient world.

Esther

Esther was probably in her teens, or—at the most—in her early twenties, when she willingly risked her life for the sake of her people the Jews.[11] Haman, a corrupt leader serving in the court of King Xerxes, had convinced the king to approve his plan to exterminate all the Jewish people living in exile in Babylon. As the favored wife of Xerxes, Esther was the only one who had any chance of appealing to the king to save the Jews. But she needed the support and encouragement of her uncle Mordecai. Her strategy was clever, creative, and very dangerous. After fasting and praying for three days with her people, this young queen of Babylon approached King Xerxes in his inner palace court without invitation. By doing this Esther was taking an enormous risk, knowing that she faced certain death unless the king himself chose to ignore this break in protocol and save her. But Esther's prayers—and those of her people—were answered, and God miraculously intervened. Instead of having her killed for approaching him in his inner court, the king held out his golden scepter to Esther, providing her with immunity to remain in his court and make her request. She simply invited the king to a banquet in his honor, which he attended. It was at this banquet that Esther was able to expose the duplicity of Haman and prevent the annihilation of God's people.

A Few Others

When Jeremiah was called to be a prophet in Judah, he pointed out to God that he was not qualified for the job because of his youth, saying, "I do not know how to speak; I am only a child."[12] But it would appear that God wanted Jeremiah in spite of—or maybe because of—his youthful exuberance and fledgling faith. Jeremiah's faith was clearly evident when he took on the difficult assignment God gave him, even though he believed that he was way too young for the job. Like many young leaders in the Bible, Jeremiah's faith and belief in God was much bigger than his faith and belief in himself.

Mary of Nazareth was a girl in her midteens when she was chosen by God to give birth to the Savior of the world. She simply trusted and accepted God's will for her to have a baby out of wedlock, never once questioning God's plan for her life, stating, "I am the Lord's servant . . . May it be to me as you have said."[13]

Although the ages of Jesus' disciples were never revealed in the New Testament, most biblical commentators concur that the disciples were young men—probably in their twenties—when they were called by Jesus to follow Him and establish the early church. The disciples certainly exhibited all the attributes of young leaders—naiveté, exuberance, faith, commitment, idealism, passion—that God consistently deploys in achieving His purposes.

Young Leaders in Church History

As with biblical history, the history of the church is replete with examples of young people being used by God to lead miraculous and strategic initiatives in mission and ministry.

James Hudson Taylor

At the age of seventeen, after reading an evangelistic tract, James Hudson Taylor gave his life to Christ. A few months later Taylor committed himself to missionary service in China and spent the next three years preparing for his "calling" by studying medicine, Mandarin, Greek, Hebrew, and Latin. On September 19, 1853, at the age of twenty-one, Taylor departed England for China driven by a vision to reach a nation for Christ. During his fifty-one years of missionary service, Taylor established the China Inland Mission (CIM), was responsible for bringing eight hundred missionaries to China, and along with his fellow workers was credited with leading thirty thousand Chinese nationals to Christ by the time he died at age seventy-three.

Taylor was known for his youthful exuberance and innovative and creative approach to mission. As with many young Christian pioneers, he was soundly criticized and rejected by the church leaders of his time. But he doggedly pursued the vision that God had given him. He was renowned for his cultural sensitivity—wearing native Chinese clothing, even though this was rare among missionaries of that time. Under his leadership, CIM was unapologetically nondenominational in practice and accepted members from all Protestant groups. These included single women, individuals from the working class, and even multinational recruits.

Ruth Tucker summarizes well Taylor's accomplishments in her book *From Jerusalem to Irian Jaya*: "No other missionary in

the nineteen centuries since the apostle Paul has had a wider
vision and has carried out a more systematized plan of evange-
lizing a broad geographical area than Hudson Taylor."[14]

The Protestant Missionary Movement
One of the greatest missionary movements in church history
was the Protestant missionary movement of North America in
the nineteenth and twentieth centuries. Thousands of missionaries, most in their early twenties, ventured out from North
America to the far corners of the world, eventually resulting
in the gospel being shared with tens of millions of previously
"unreached" peoples. The roots of this movement can be traced
to an impromptu prayer meeting held when a group of five
students at Williams College in Massachusetts hid together
under a haystack to shelter from a storm.

During this "haystack" prayer meeting, these zealous young
students focused on the need for awakening interest in foreign
missions among their peers. Their leader, Samuel Mills, ex-
horted his companions with the words that later became their
motto: "We can do this if we will." They committed themselves
to foreign missionary service, and they challenged other students on their campus to commit their lives to missions along
with them. Then they traveled across the U.S., going from campus to campus sharing their vision for missions. The movement
grew exponentially until the whole church in North America
was affected by their missionary vision.

Other Young Mission Pioneers
Throughout the modern mission movement students have been
at the forefront of pioneering missionary efforts. The Student
Volunteer Movement sent out thousands of college students

from North America and Britain in the late nineteenth and early twentieth centuries. Their catchphrase was "The evangelization of the world in this generation."

Another example of a youth-led mission was the great student revival in North America in the twentieth century, when students from colleges such as Asbury College traveled all over North America, sharing what God had done in their lives and triggering revivals wherever they went.

Today's modern mission movements such as Youth With A Mission, Youth for Christ, Operation Mobilization, Navigators, and Campus Crusade for Christ were all started by young leaders in their early twenties—Loren Cunningham, Torrey Johnson, Billy Graham, George Verwer, Dawson Trotman, and Bill Bright.

These young courageous leaders—along with a host of missionary firebrands of the past two hundred years—were all marked by their absolute commitment to reaching the unreached and to establishing God's kingdom in the remotest and farthest corners of the world. They were literally prepared to give their lives in pursuit of the call of Jesus to "make disciples of all nations." In fact, in the early 1800s many missionaries shipped their goods to the mission field in coffins because they knew they would most likely die abroad from disease or at the hand of the people they were trying to reach. Such passion, sacrifice, and love for those without Christ resulted in an unprecedented growth of the church worldwide and ultimately the salvation of hundreds of millions of unreached people.

The Next Wave of Mission

As globalization and modern technology shrink our world, we are presented with a new seascape that contains amazing possibilities for communicating the love, grace, forgiveness, and hope of the gospel. We live in a global society that is experiencing a famine of unconditional sacrificial love; a world where people have lost the art of relationship; a world that is rife with relativism and in which absolutes and foundational truth are often rejected because they either have no place in post-Christian humanism, or they are associated with repressive regimes or leadership.

People are searching—they are searching for the truth; they are searching for love; they are searching for relationship; they are searching for meaning and purpose; they are searching for security—they are searching for Jesus! In the words of Jesus, "The harvest is plentiful, but the workers are few. Ask the Lord of the harvest, therefore, to send out workers into his harvest field."[15]

The world is ready for the next wave of mission. In the context of globalization and modern technology, the potential impact of this building wave is inestimable. In the same way young people were at the forefront of all the major mission movements of the past, I believe that once again they will be at the forefront of a tidal wave that is going to sweep across this planet in the next few decades. The question remains for the rest of us who have been part of the last wave for a long or short time: Will we stand in the way of the wave, get out of the way of the wave, or be part of the *next wave* of mission?

NOTES

1. Short spontaneous video interviews with young people in the community.

2. A simulation game is a mixture of a game of skill, a game of chance, and a game of strategy, which results in a simulation of complex real-life situations.

3. Canberra is the capital territory of Australia.

4. 1 Samuel 17

5. 1 Samuel 17:50

6. 2 Chronicles 34

7. 2 Chronicles 34:19,27

8. Daniel 3

9. Daniel 3:17-18

10. Daniel 3:27

11. Esther 4:16

12. Jeremiah 1:6

13. Luke 1:38

14. Ruth Tucker, *From Jerusalem to Irian Jaya* (Grand Rapids: Zondervan, 1983), p. 173.

15. Luke 10:2

CHAPTER THREE

TECHNOLOGY, GLOBALIZATION, AND MISSION

Irene Lin was on her way to a very successful professional career. She had just graduated with a master's degree in communication from one of the most prestigious universities in Taiwan, and she had big plans for the future. But God had other plans for this creative young leader.

As Irene started to map out her career path, God intervened and redirected her vision to reach the young people of her nation. After exploring the possibilities and challenges of her vision for some months, God led Irene to Youth for Christ. Irene was sure YFC was where God wanted her, but the YFC Taiwan ministry had been through a difficult period, resulting in the loss of all of the full-time staff and most of the volunteers. Nearly all of the YFC ministry programs had ceased operation, and funding had fallen off to such an extent that they could hardly maintain the few remaining programs, let alone support expansion. But Irene's calling was not dissuaded by the state of the YFC ministry or the lack of resources. If YFC was the best vehicle to accomplish her vision, then YFC would have to be fixed as a preliminary step in pursuing her vision.

At the time that the YFC Taiwan ministry was going through this difficult period, I was serving as the YFC Asia Pacific Area Director. Due to the fragility of the ministry, I arranged to visit Taiwan to consult with the national board. When I met with the board, I recognized all the signs of a very discouraged but highly committed group of people, who were willing to do whatever was necessary to rebuild the ministry. We discussed a number of options for restructuring and recruiting new leadership, but nothing seemed workable. In the end I asked the board members if they had any ideas at all as to what strategy we could employ to reactivate the ministry and impact youth with the gospel. It was at this point in our conversation that they mentioned Irene, stating that they thought she had some good ideas. They asked me to meet with her and assess whether her ideas had any merit.

By the time I met Irene, God had expanded her vision for reaching her nation, and she had developed a comprehensive strategy around that vision. She excitedly shared an overview of her strategy with me. Her plan was to build a virtual world and to use this world to reach and make disciples of the young people of Taiwan.

I must admit, I was skeptical at first, and I expressed my reservations to Irene. I explained to her that although we use the Internet as a ministry tool in other nations, our Internet programs were always just an adjunct or support for our face-to-face outreach and discipleship ministry. I just couldn't see how she—or anyone—could use the Internet and a website as a primary "stand-alone" ministry strategy and achieve the level of relational connection that was necessary for making disciples of Jesus.

But Irene was undaunted by my lack of enthusiasm. She presented me with her documented strategy, meticulously translated into English. As she animatedly walked me through the specifics of her strategy, explaining her rationale for a web-based ministry, I began to see Taiwan through her eyes, finally appreciating the genius of her unique approach to youth mission.

Obviously there were many things I didn't know about the Taiwanese culture and society, and Irene was highly motivated to educate me. She told me that from grade four in elementary school, Taiwanese children commence technology-infused classes. By the time students reach junior high school, about 80 percent of them have become habitual users of the Internet. Irene further explained to me that in the context of a rigid and structured society, Taiwanese teenagers are attracted by the freedom of the Internet. They can escape into a wonderful fantasy world, be anyone they choose to be, and attain a sense of empowerment that allows them to escape the futility and limitations of the real world. They use the Internet to find friends, play computer games, build a new identity, and experience community. In recent years the Internet café has become their favorite place of entertainment. Many teenagers become addicted to the virtual world. They are exploring all the freedoms of the Internet and experiencing all its shortcomings.

To provide further evidence of the appropriateness of her strategy, Irene showed me a newspaper article. The story was on the front page of the primary English newspaper in Taipei. It was about Internet cafés and the addictive behavior of the young people who frequented them. Teenagers would go into these cafés on Friday evening and would not come out until

Sunday night, or even Monday morning. Occasionally, users of the cafés would be so engrossed in the virtual world that they would forget to eat and drink, faint at the keyboard, and end up in an ambulance taking them to the hospital to be re-hydrated. The article reported that the Taiwanese government was so concerned about this problem that it was considering introducing legislation that would ban young people under the age of eighteen from being in an Internet café after 11:00 p.m. With this article in mind, it was obvious that Irene was explor-ing a new angle of a core ministry strategy YFC has always employed—go where the young people are!

After working through the strategy and reading this news-paper article, I raised my next concern with Irene, and that was the enormity of the task of building such a complex website. I asked her if she realized how many people and how much money it took to develop a "virtual world." It shouldn't have surprised me that she was prepared for this question and had an answer to this challenge. The next day she introduced me to her "team." This team consisted of five young people, all who were prepared to give up their careers and join Irene in YFC. They were graduates in various disciplines, including graphic design, computer science, and programming. I realized my res-ervations were about three steps behind Irene and her team. I was struggling with the "how" and they were already answer-ing the "who" questions.

In the face of such overwhelming enthusiasm and impeccable planning—not to mention the lack of any other viable ministry alternatives—I really had no choice but to support Irene and her team. In no time at all Irene and the YFC Taiwan board raised all the funds they required to build the infrastructure to house the website. In less than a year, working with her team of brilliant young professionals, Irene created "Walei World,"[1] a virtual environment for reaching young people.

Walei World consists of a universe of spinning planets. Members begin their journey into the world by first selecting a planet, a nation, and then some land, all with the objective of building a home and becoming part of the Walei community. Dedicated planets are also included in the website, whose mission is to provide entertainment, counseling, and advice to the residents of the other planets. The houses are designed with interiors that look like spaceships. Every member's house is equipped with a complete interactive system—including a bulletin board, a diary, a mailbox, a pen-pal system, instant messaging, a virtual café chat room, and a "special topics" discussion area—all to encourage members to communicate with each other and develop friendships.

The site is designed to provide opportunities for non-Christian members to get to know some Christian friends and learn about the Christian value system in a nonconfrontational and sensitive environment. This encourages them to open their hearts to share their problems and seek help.

Irene recruited Christian teachers and university and seminary students to serve as the "Christian friends" of the Walei members. She set up training programs to equip these volunteers to serve as area leaders. Their primary responsibilities include caring for other members, developing site content, and encouraging member participation in site activities. The area leaders also engage in cultural and religious discussions with the members. They are called the "Guardian Angel Team" and are the core evangelists of the site, reaching out to non-Christian student members through friendship, dialogue, counsel, and support. Guardian Angels are available twenty-four hours a day, every day of the week, for any member to call on for advice, help, or companionship. Irene and some of her board members also trained a group of core counselors, whose mission is to help, members who want to know more about Jesus and who wish to discuss issues of faith and life with someone before they make a commitment.

A "Secret Counselor Mailbox" was set up and a team of "Secret Counselors"—Christian ministers, counselors, and teachers—were recruited to respond daily to the messages from members with personal problems that include abuse, relationships, family issues, academics, and sexuality.

In the first few months of operation the Walei website signed up more than 15,000 members. Of these, 72 percent were non-Christians, without any church affiliation. Irene continued to populate the website with hundreds of Christian volunteers recruited and trained to serve as Guardian Angels and Secret Counselors, reaching out to Walei members.

In the first full year of operation, here's what happened: Just over 20,000 young people joined Walei World; 1,880 young people became Christians; approximately 4,000 young people received counseling for other issues; 28 face-to-face outreach programs were conducted (such as computer camps and youth events); and the Walei team worked with 281 public schools and 33 local churches.

Walei World (as of 2007) has a membership of approximately 40,000 regular users, hundreds of volunteers, and is seeing thousands of young people come to faith in Christ each year. At the age of thirty, Irene was appointed as the National Director of YFC Taiwan.

The Potential of Modern Technology

Irene is a great example of a young leader who, because of her unshakable faith, creativity, youthful naiveté, connectedness to the youth community, and never-say-never approach to life and ministry, was able to achieve amazing things for God. But Irene's story does more than provide us with another example of the value of allowing young people the freedom to lead; it is an eye-opening example of the enormous potential of modern technology to be used as a platform to reach the world with the gospel of Jesus Christ. With their specialized understanding of modern technology, Irene and her team were able to harness all of its power to reach the young people of Taiwan.

The advance of technology has caught many people by surprise. Things that a few decades ago would have been placed in the realm of "science fiction" are now part of our everyday life. Cars follow voice commands. GPS devices talk, directing you to your destination. Robots recognize different people, carry out complex conversations, serve as secretaries, monitor the condition of the sick, and function as house sitters and domestic helpers. Forensic medicine enables police to identify criminals from microscopic samples of DNA. Medical advances make it possible to conduct multiple organ transplants, including face and hand transplants. Communication systems have the capacity to communicate with billions of people at one time. Satellite technology allows us to connect with anyone, anywhere in the world, no matter how remote they may be. Electronic storage systems make it possible for anyone with a midranged computer to store all the information from all the books in an average public library.

I can now sit in a departure lounge at an airport in Europe and, using a tiny camera attached to the top of my laptop and wireless technology, I can have a video meeting with one of my staff who is sitting in the basement of his home in Colorado in the U.S. We can share and edit documents, send files to each other, including sound and video clips, and chat face-to-face for hours.

The World Is Flat

Thomas Friedman, in his best-selling book *The World Is Flat*,[2] provides a brilliant overview of how advances in modern technology, communication, and marketing have flattened the world. Friedman explains how the world is rapidly shrinking and how geographical, language, and cultural boundaries are becoming more and more blurred. Never before have we had the resources, technology, and accessibility now available to us to effectively and instantaneously communicate and connect with people all over the world.

To describe how globalization has flattened the world, Friedman uses the example of the Asian computer company Lenovo. Lenovo has a strategic alliance with the U.S.-owned IBM and is responsible for the manufacture of all IBM personal computers. This Chinese-owned company's headquarters is located in New York, but its primary manufacturing operation is in Beijing. Its research centers are in China, the United States, and Japan, and its sales centers are located in major cities all over the world. Lenovo has a Chinese chairman, an American CEO, an American CPO, and a Chinese CFO, and it is listed on the Hong Kong stock exchange.

Much of Microsoft's research and development is now done by Chinese computer engineers, all PhD-qualified and living in

Dalian, China. Bill Gates said that within just a couple of years of its opening in 1998, Microsoft Research Asia had become the most productive research arm in the Microsoft system "in terms of the quality of the ideas that they are turning out."[3]

Many U.S. personal tax returns are prepared in India. Because of the advantages of the time zone differential, tax returns can be dropped off at a U.S. tax agent's office in the evening, be sent immediately to India utilizing scanners and electronic forms, be processed by Indian accountants in Bangalore in regular business hours, and be ready for the client in the U.S. the next morning.

A Shrinking World

When I was in Rwanda recently, I traveled with a team of East African young leaders up to the northern town of Gisenyi, which is located on the border of the Democratic Republic of the Congo. We were staying in an old guesthouse. While I was having dinner in the dining room of the guesthouse, one of the serving staff turned on the television. I was stunned with what I saw on the screen. Here I was in one of the remotest towns in Africa and I was watching the Commonwealth Games broadcast live from Australia. The bizarre thing was that prior to this trip, I was lamenting the fact that I couldn't get the Commonwealth Games on my own television in Denver, Colorado. I had to travel all the way to Gisenyi to see these games.

After the report on the games finished, the staff changed the channel, and on came *The O.C.*, an American television series about life in Orange County, California. The hotel staff were mesmerized by the program. As they worked around the tables, they couldn't take their eyes off the screen. I was disturbed as I watched these young Rwandans absorb the rampant materialism and deplorable moral values portrayed by this program. The next morning a French drama series was playing. At lunchtime we all watched the World Cup football (soccer) from Germany. In the two days I was in Gisenyi, the guesthouse staff had been exposed to the sport, culture, values, and language of four Western nations from vastly separated geographical locations of the world.

Modern technology had brought the world to these Rwandans living in an extremely remote part of East Africa. A large, rusty satellite dish on the roof of an old guesthouse building had become a portal to the world beyond Rwanda. Many of these guesthouse staff had probably never been outside of their local cultural and geographical context, and yet they already had extensive exposure to at least the media's version of the culture, values, music, social structure, language, sport, and geography of many other nations of the world.

Young People and Technology

Young people have an insatiable appetite for new technology. They are always looking for the latest upgrades in software and hardware and can't wait until the next version comes out. On the other hand, we older users of technology usually breathe a big sigh of frustration when technology companies bring out a new version of software or hardware. It takes us a year to master even the basic functions of the programs, phone, computer, and PDA that we are currently using. Then they bring out a new version of everything, and we are faced with another year of trial-and-error to get on top of these "upgraded" versions.

The adaptability and techno-savvy of young people is astounding. They seem to have an innate ability to master all the features of new products and programs after just using them once or twice. So when it comes to evangelism, ministry, and mission, young people are ideally suited to harness the full potential of the technology and communication systems that have flattened our world.

In 1998, when the Internet was just beginning to be used by the broader community, I was fascinated with how quickly my twelve-year-old son, Michael, mastered new technology and stretched our home computer system to the limits of its capacity. He spent a lot of time on "the Net," mostly talking to people around the world in various "chat rooms." He would often conduct conversations with six people at once, sometimes as many as ten. He quickly developed friendships with other young people all over the world.

Michael and a friend set up their own chat room. They called the room "Aussie Clean Teens" (interesting name when he wasn't yet a teen himself). They were getting tired of the foul language that people constantly used in chat sessions, and they wanted a room that was free of this language problem.

One day Michael and his friend were chatting with a seventeen-year-old guy in Canada whom they had met in their chat room. This guy was experiencing all kinds of problems in his family and other relationships and was clearly very depressed. While chatting, he said that he was so sick of life that he was going to end it there and then. He told Michael and his friend that he had a razor blade and was going to slit his wrists. And that's exactly what he did, providing a graphic description of how the blood was running all over the desk and keyboard as he was typing what he thought were his last words.

Michael and his friend immediately contacted someone who was online and fortunately lived close to this young man. They asked him to go around to this guy's house to check on him. When he arrived at the house, he found that Michael's friend had indeed carried out his threat. He called for help and the paramedics arrived in time to save this young man's life. The teen was back online after a couple of days. Michael—along with his other friends from around the world—was able to help this guy work through the issues in his life to a degree where he became far more stable.

Michael's experience is a vivid example of how globalization has changed our world. Using the Internet, a twelve-year-old boy in Melbourne, Australia, was able to build a close enough friendship with a seventeen-year-old in Canada to be able to be instrumental in saving him from an attempt on his own life. Technology has come a long way since 1998, and the ability of young people to build relationships and connect with each other worldwide has increased significantly.

■ ■ ■ ■ ■ ■ ■

It is hard for us who have grown into the technological world—as opposed to those who have grown up in it—to understand how this generation can establish and maintain meaningful relationships on the Internet and in the virtual world. But the fact is that they do; they can develop very close relationships with people they have never met face-to-face. Irene and her Walei World team provide convincing evidence that you can reach young people for Jesus in cyber space. The follow-up and discipleship programs of Walei are extensive and very effective; not only are young people introduced to Jesus on the Web, but they are also nurtured and mentored in their newfound faith.

Globalization has opened up a huge array of opportunities for outreach and discipleship. It is now possible to have multiple staff and volunteers in various geographical and cultural settings worldwide, all working together efficiently for the cause of Christ. The apostle Paul used the cutting-edge technology of his time when he employed the mail system of the Roman Empire to deliver his letters to widely separated churches. He even used young people such as Timothy, Titus, and Silas to deliver his messages. The basic principle still works. Distance has often become a non-factor. Opportunities for people to get involved in supporting and mentoring young leaders across the world are numerous. Prayer mentoring, peer mentoring, coaching, and teaching are no longer limited to geographical proximity. Assigning a mentor from the U.S., England, or Australia to a young leader in Africa, Asia, or Latin America is a feasible option.

Mission Partnership and Support

I recall when I was a child watching my mother write letters to missionaries in various nations around the world. Because of the very expensive postal charges associated with sending mail to remote parts of the world, in an attempt to keep the weight of these letters to a minimum, my mother wrote letters on very thin "airmail" paper in the smallest handwriting she could produce. She then took the letters to the post office to arrange for their delivery. At the post office they weighed the letters and charged her per ounce to send them to their destination. Several months—sometimes four or five months—went by before my mother received a reply.

Today, my mother sits at the computer, and in thirty minutes can type a lengthy e-mail and send it to the missionaries she corresponds with. Sometimes within an hour she will have a reply; at the very least she generally hears from those she e-mailed by the next day. Not only is my mother now able to communicate instantaneously with her missionary friends, she can also share photos and short video clips. The world has flattened to such a degree that rather than feeling the separation of thousands of miles from those she cares about on the mission field, my mother feels part of their daily lives, with an intimate connection that engenders a very real sense of partnership and participation in their ministry.

World Mission in the Context of Globalization
Korean Mission in New Zealand

God is raising up young mission-minded people all over the world who look at mission from a global perspective. This has led to mission occurring well beyond the scope of traditional mission models and in traditional mission fields. Nations that were once viewed as "receiving" nations are now "sending" nations, and sending nations have now become mission fields for the traditional receiving nations. Roles within the global mission of the church of Christ are now continually ebbing and flowing.

A classic example of this occurred back in 2003 when Lee Ho Taek, a young pastor and YFC leader in Korea, was challenged to look beyond his own nation's borders to reach "unreached" young people in another nation. Ho Taek's exploration of mission opportunities finally resulted in moving with his young family to Auckland, New Zealand.

Why would God send a young Korean leader with a passion to reach "unreached" young people to Auckland, New Zealand? Surprisingly, Auckland is a city that has a very large Korean community, comprised of a youth population of twenty thousand Korean young people. YFC New Zealand had identified this Korean youth community as one of the "unreached" people groups in their nation. They had been praying specifically for three years for someone to accept the challenge of leading a ministry to reach these young people. All attempts by local YFC staff to establish a ministry had failed due to the significant cultural and language barriers that needed to be crossed to effectively connect with the Korean young people and the Korean community leaders.

Ho Taek provided the key that unlocked the door to effective mission. One of the senior YFC staff was assigned the task of assisting Ho Taek to establish the ministry. By combining the expertise and programs of YFC New Zealand with the cultural sensitivity and leadership of Ho Taek, YFC has been able to reach thousands of Korean young people in Auckland, as well as in other regions of New Zealand.

Central Asia

Another example of this globalization of mission is YFC's development of ministry in Central Asia. A few years ago when I was serving as the YFC Asia Pacific Area Director, our area leadership team felt a strong call from God to develop a ministry in Central Asia. We identified this as a strategic region of the world where YFC had no mission presence. We conducted a number of investigative trips, visiting several different nations. Eventually we selected a nation that we felt provided the most viable geographical, political, and social environment for us to establish an effective local youth ministry, as well as provide us with a beachhead to develop further mission across the whole Central Asian region.

One of the challenges we faced in establishing our ministry in this moderate Muslim Russian-speaking nation was that there was very little youth ministry being conducted by the local church or any other mission agencies. Targeted youth ministry wasn't on anyone's radar screen. Realizing our vision would require us to send in people to support, train, equip, and mobilize local people, we initially planned to send in some experienced youth ministry staff from the U.S., Australia, and other Western nations. However, as we developed a strategy around sending in Westerners, it became obvious it was going to take a long time to get the ministry established. People coming from Western nations first had to raise support—and this involved a significant financial challenge—as well as learn Russian. Then they would spend a substantial amount of time adapting to the culture, further improving on their Russian, and building relationships with local believers, community leaders, and young people. The whole process was going to take about three years before any significant ministry could occur.

It wasn't long before we realized that sending in Westerners was not a good strategy. It was obvious we had to find another way, and after a little more investigation of possibilities, we realized that we had an ideal recruitment and sending base in Eastern Europe. The YFC ministry in Ukraine is one of YFC's strongest and most effective ministries in the world. Ukraine—being a former Soviet nation—has a very similar culture and social environment to the nations in Central Asia, and of course the *lingua franca*[4] in Ukraine and Central Asia is Russian.

We recruited a number of young Ukrainian leaders, and trained and equipped them in the local YFC ministry in Ukraine. It was an enormous advantage training these young leaders within a well-established youth ministry in a very similar culture to the culture of the new country to which they would be going.

After a year of training, these young leaders were sent into Central Asia. They quickly adapted to the culture and local environment and in the first few weeks made meaningful contact with both local youth and local churches. Their "bridging" work began almost immediately. In the first month they assisted in conducting a summer camping ministry for local youth. They were able to reach over a thousand young people, and saw around two hundred of these young people give their lives to Jesus.

After returning from the camping program, two of the YFC leaders introduced eighty new Christians into a local church. Needless to say the local church was at a loss to know how to cater to eighty new youth, eager for spiritual input. So the YFC leaders offered to help run the church youth program—an offer that was gladly accepted. In the next few months many other churches in the city contacted the YFC leaders and asked for their assistance with their youth program. So in a matter of months an effective youth ministry was established in a pioneer mission environment.

A New Era of Mission

The amazing success of this Central Asian mission venture is a powerful example of how globalization has opened up the possibility for an incredibly rapid expansion of mission across the world. We no longer need to rely on Western nations to send missionaries into foreign environments where they will be hamstrung by the cultural, financial, language, and adaptation challenges associated with people trying to integrate into completely alien settings. The globalization of the church allows us to have almost instant access to any place in the world by providing a multicultural sending pool for mission and ministry.

Also, because the youth culture is the most globalized culture in the world, when like-cultured young people are sent to unreached people groups, they easily connect with local youth, and therefore are able to establish fruitful ministries very quickly. And because of the commonality and interconnectedness of the youth culture, it is far easier for young leaders to recruit others to be involved in ministry. The Central Asia team quickly mobilized local Christian youth. After only a year in the nation, they had developed an impressive team of local young people serving as volunteer leaders.

We are now presented with a completely different landscape when we consider the demographics of those involved in Christian mission. In 1990, about 91 percent of foreign missionaries came from Western nations. By 2000, this percentage had decreased to 79 percent. During the last decade of the twentieth century, foreign missionary sending from non-Western countries increased threefold, in spite of very difficult global economic conditions.[5]

This trend has continued with significant increases in the number of missionaries being sent out from non-Western nations. For example, the church in South Korea now sends out more missionaries than any other nation except the U.S., with almost thirteen thousand South Korean missionaries serving long-term in countries around the world.

In 1973, there were 3,411 non-Western, cross-cultural missionaries in the world. Reliable estimates now put that number at 103,000.[6] Scott Moreau, chair of Intercultural Studies at Wheaton Graduate School, says, "The day of Western missionary dominance is over, not because Western missionaries have died off, but because the rest of the world has caught the vision and is engaged and energized."[7]

Training and Education in a Flat World

In response to these developments and in partnership with some other Christian education and mission organizations, YFC has launched an online university to assist in the training and development of staff, volunteers, and church leaders worldwide. Students can log on anywhere in the world and take classes in apologetics, theology, public speaking, biblical studies, and youth ministry, downloading PDF files and lecture notes. If they have a broadband connection, they can receive whole lectures via a video stream, complete with supportive video clips of biblical locations or other relevant material. They can take exams online and at the end of the course, they can download a certificate with their name and course details on it—including the signature of the university president—print their certificate on a color printer, frame it, and place it on the wall of their office or home. A whole course can be completed without having to travel, navigate complex and lengthy visa application processes, disrupt ministry and family life, or pay enormous sums for airfares, accommodations, and college fees.

Along with a coalition of Christian colleges and ministries, YFC is also currently developing a worldwide training and Christian education program that will offer accredited college diplomas and degrees to young people all over the world in their own local geographical and culture context. The courses and educational programs will be delivered to the regional training centers and to individual students via the Internet. The plan is to have sixty thousand students worldwide within ten years.

Each of these students will be assigned a mentor to disciple and support them in their development as a leader and follower of Jesus. (This may well be where *you* come in!) The only viable way of providing mentors for so many young leaders will be to recruit them from all over the world and have a majority of them support the students via the Internet. Prior to the advent of modern technology and communication systems, we would not have been able to even imagine doing what we are doing with this education and leadership development program, let alone have the capacity to do it.

Friedman's Challenge

In *The World Is Flat*, Thomas Friedman concludes by observing that there is nothing we can do to stop this flattening of the world, but we can manage it, for better or for worse. We can flourish in this flat world, but it is going to take the "right imagination" and the "right motivation." He throws out a challenge to the young people of his generation to be "the generation of optimists, the generation with more dreams than memories, the generation that wakes up each morning and not only imagines that things can be better but also acts on that imagination every day."[8]

This is a worthy challenge, and one that vibrant, Christ-focused young believers are already enthusiastically accepting, as they download and harness the power of modern technology and make the most of the unprecedented opportunities offered by a rapidly shrinking, globalized world.

NOTES

1. *Walei* means "cool" in Mandarin.
2. Thomas Friedman, *The World Is Flat* (New York: Farrar, Straus and Giroux, 2005).
3. Friedman, p. 266.
4. *Lingua franca* is the "common language."
5. David Taylor, "*Operation World 2001* Reveals Emerging Global Trends," *Mission Frontier* (Dec 2001), published by U.S. Center for World Mission.
6. Rob Moll, "Missions Incredible," *Christianity Today* (Mar 2006), pp. 28, 30.
7. Scott Moreau, quoted in Moll, p. 30.
8. Friedman, p. 469.

CHAPTER FOUR

PEER-TO-PEER
EVANGELISM

Teresa grew up in a small country town a couple of hours' drive southeast of Melbourne, Australia. When she was in her mid-teens, some of her friends invited her to a Youth for Christ event called "Happening." Happening was a weekend youth festival held twice a year at a convention center in the Dandenong Mountains, attracting up to five thousand young people.

Teresa was not a Christian. She didn't really have any idea who Jesus is or what it means to be a follower of Jesus. She came to Happening because her friends told her about the great music, the thousands of young people that turned up, and the great opportunity to meet guys. But God had other plans for Teresa apart from having a good time and meeting guys. Through the music, messages, and the testimony of her friends, Teresa was confronted with the claims of Jesus Christ. At the Saturday evening program she handed her life over to Christ.

At the time I was the Executive Director of Youth for Christ in Melbourne. I hadn't been in the role long and was trying to implement some new follow-up strategies for the young people who responded at YFC events and programs. One of the things I decided to do was to write a personal letter to all the young people who gave their life to Jesus at the Happening events. Teresa received one of these letters.

In the letter I asked the young people to write back to me and let me know how they were getting on in their newfound faith. Teresa was one of the young people who responded to my letter. In her letter she shared how excited she was to have found Jesus. She told me a little of how her life had changed since the Happening, and how she was now sharing her faith with her friends. She went on to explain that after the event, she went immediately to her friend's house to share with her friend about her newfound faith. At first her friend had no idea what she was talking about. But over a period of two weeks, Teresa explained more about her faith in Jesus to her friend, and she was just writing to let me know that her friend had also become a Christian.

As you can imagine, I was thrilled with this news. I immediately wrote back and encouraged Teresa in her walk with Jesus, and celebrated with her about the salvation of her friend. A couple of months later I received another letter from Teresa. She shared how she was now involved in a local church and was studying the Bible and growing in her faith. But then she went on to state that the main reason for her letter was to share some great news with me: Twenty-three of her other friends had now become Christians! I was astounded. This girl, who had only been a Christian for three months, had already led twenty-three of her friends to Jesus.

Not long after she became a Christian, Teresa wrote this poem and sent it to me:

My life was once a lonely one
No purpose could I find
To make my life so meaningful,
So fulfilled in soul and mind.
I searched the mountains far and wide
For truth of why I'm here,
Many rivers did I cross
And hardship did appear.

While struggling to fight the storm
That raged within my heart,
I found some friends who showed the light
Which overcame the dark.
Then with your word they showed your love,
Then took me by the hand
And led me to the Mighty One,
Their Lord, Savior, and friend.

I spoke your name, and sought your love,
Jesus, please forgive.
I love you, Lord, I praise your name,
For you, I want to live.
Take my life and mold me
So that others may see you.
Thank you for forgiving me
And for your love so true.

Now I walk through valleys green
And peacefulness is there.

And when I face the raging storm
You give me strength to bear.
The meaninglessness in my life
Has faded far away.
For you I live, to spread your word
And love you more each day.

I pray for those who face the storm
And have not made it through
That they may soon realize your love
And live only for you.
Jesus, I thank you, Lord,
for everything you do,
For loving me, forgiving me,
Remaining a friend so true.

Teresa went on to be a key leader in her church, and the last I heard, she was preparing for full-time mission work.

Teresa's genuine, authentic, and simple faith made her infectious. Her story is a great example of a strategic principle that I see continually demonstrated in youth ministry all over the world: *When it comes to reaching young people with the gospel, the most effective agents of Jesus are other young people.* They are entrenched and accepted in the culture, they speak the language of youth, and they have daily contact with those whom they are trying to reach.

The Importance of Reaching People in Their Youth

Motivating, empowering, and equipping young people to reach their peers are essential elements in order for the church to reach the world and fulfill the Great Commission.[1] Surveys conducted in the U.S. have continually demonstrated that close to 80 percent of "born again" Christians committed their life to Jesus before they reached the age of twenty-one.[2] Anecdotal evidence indicates that this U.S. statistic is reflected in many other nations across the world. I have conducted "straw polls" among groups of Christians in a wide variety of cultural, geographical, and ethnic contexts, asking them at what age they gave their life to Jesus. I consistently find that over 80 percent of the respondents became Christians in their teens.

If most people who are Christians in the world today made a commitment to Christ when they were in their youth, then surely it is not unreasonable to propose that if we are to be effective in reaching the world and making long-term disciples of Jesus, we need to focus our efforts on reaching young people. If young people are most effective at reaching other young people, then it would also seem obvious that a key element in following Jesus' command to "go and make disciples of all nations"[3] must involve the mobilization of youth to reach their peers.

The Art of Listening

Australian journalist Max Harris once said, "Christians are a dim, ego-tripping minority which is dead set on telling everybody why they ought to become Christians, instead of finding out why they're not."

Unfortunately there is a lot of truth in what Max Harris says. When it comes to sharing our faith, we are generally not good listeners, particularly those of us who have been Christians for some time and have "matured" in our faith. We believe we have the answers to life's big questions, and are so intent on telling others about Jesus and the gospel that we seldom take the time to listen to their story. We tend to project to those we are trying to reach—and maybe we even believe this—that their story has little validity unless it has Jesus in it.

The thing about *new* Christians is that they have a very simple and fresh faith. Because they know they don't have all the answers, it is far easier for them to identify with the story of the people they are endeavoring to reach, and not present themselves as people who "have it all together." One of the reasons Teresa was so effective in reaching her peers was because she didn't seem to her friends as someone who was way ahead of them in her faith journey. She simply shared her story with them. And she was a great listener, validating her friends' stories by listening to them more than telling them what they needed to do.

A Surfing Evangelist

I have a number of friends in leadership roles in a ministry called Christian Surfers. For many years I was mentoring and supporting some young leaders in the movement. I had the privilege of speaking at several Christian Surfers' conferences and events. At one of these conferences I met a young surfer who hadn't been a Christian long but was already an incredibly effective evangelist. In the short time he had been a Christian, he had guided many others into a relationship with Jesus.

The surfing community is not an easy community to reach. Surfers are particularly suspicious and wary of Christians. Surfing is their religion, and their culture is characterized by free living and self-indulgence. They reject anyone who is peddling an alternate system of priorities and values. So I was eager to find out why this guy was so effective in reaching his peers.

The first thing I discovered about this surfing evangelist was that he was a very good surfer and was respected in the surfing community. So, one of the keys to his effectiveness in reaching surfers was that he was already well accepted in his peer network. Another key was, of course, that he knew the language and culture of those he was trying to reach. He had credibility in his subculture. This is a good starting point in effective peer-to-peer evangelism, but it is not enough to just "belong." You can belong but still be ineffective in reaching your peers.

This guy's secret of effectiveness was his authentic faith combined with his ability to listen. His evangelism method was very basic. He would paddle out to the back of the break where all the surfers wait for the waves. He would work his way to another surfer and ask, "Are you a Christian?" The usual reply was, "No!" Then he would simply ask, "Why not?" And then he would listen, sometimes for hours, to these fellow surfers tell why they were not Christians. After he heard their stories, he would share with them why he was a Christian. More often than not, he would end up leading them to faith in Christ, generally not in his first encounter, but after several weeks of listening and sharing.

During my many years in youth ministry, I have found that the earlier in a faith journey a young person is mobilized and equipped in evangelism, the better it is for his or her long-term effectiveness in reaching and discipling others. Equipping young people to reach their peers is best achieved by providing a framework for evangelism that encourages them to draw on their strengths, especially their connectedness to the youth community, and their innate ability to share their life stories.

3Story Evangelism

Youth for Christ USA has a very effective evangelism strategy and associated training program for young people called

"3Story" evangelism. I have seen the principles of 3Story applied across an extensive range of cultural, ethnic, religious, and social contexts. In every case it has been remarkably effective in equipping young people to share their faith and to help them in the process of introducing other young people to Jesus. The reason why 3Story is so effective is because it equips young people to be great listeners. It provides them with a framework to listen to other young people's stories, share their own story, and then share God's story. It is not so much a method of evangelism as a lifestyle that helps young people develop a deeper understanding of their relationship with God, and how this relationship intersects with others' life stories.

Of course, these principles of listening and sharing naturally about our relationship with Jesus apply to all who follow Him, not only young people. When I meet people for the first time and have a chance to chat with them for a while, I endeavor to draw out their story. I ask them about their family, their job, where they live, where they grew up, and so on. And as our conversation progresses and I have the opportunity to share my own story with them, it is not long before I will tell them about my wife, Jenny, and our three children. We are a very close family, and next to Jesus, my wife and children are the most important people in my life. So I can't help but talk about them as a natural extension of who I am.

People are generally comfortable when I talk about my family. But I know from experience that many people—particularly if they are not Christians—are not comfortable talking about Jesus and issues of faith. So I am very careful not to "force" Jesus into a conversation. But just as I can't help talking about my family because they are so much a part of my life, eventually I will find myself talking about my faith and relationship with Jesus. He is the focal point of my life and has so much impact on who I am and what I do that it is impossible for me to share much about myself without my faith and relationship with Jesus naturally coming into the conversation.

No Secret Christianity

In my teenage years I was greatly influenced by the music and ministry of Keith Green. I recall watching a video of Keith performing in a park before tens of thousands of young people. In the middle of a song he suddenly stopped, looked out across the vast crowd of youth, and stated, "If you are not known as a Christian at school, at work, or at home, then you are probably not one." Keith was someone who lived and breathed his faith, and everyone who encountered him was captivated by his love for Jesus. He couldn't see how someone could be a genuine disciple of Jesus and keep it a secret.

When we commit our lives to Christ, our primary relationship becomes our relationship with Jesus. This relationship by its very nature should supersede and significantly impact any other relationship we have in life. Sharing Jesus with others we encounter in our day-to-day lives should be a natural extension of who we are and a by-product of our relationship with Him. Rather than forcing Jesus into a story-sharing conversation, Jesus should be there as naturally and as unobtrusively as our family and friends.

In Matthew 5 Jesus commands us not to keep our relationship with Him a secret, stating, "You are the light of the world. A city on a hill cannot be hidden. Neither do people light a lamp and put it under a bowl. Instead they put it on its stand,

and it gives light to everyone in the house. In the same way, let your light shine before men."[4]

If Jesus truly is the number one priority in our lives, then it really will be impossible for us to be a "secret" Christian. Not only will we be unable to keep Jesus out of our conversation, He will shine through our lives with such intensity that those we meet in our day-to-day lives will not be able to ignore Him. In fact, it is just as well that we are not reliant on only our own words to convince others to follow Christ, because then all people would ever get to see would be us. Reaching others, particularly young people, involves more than just talking about Jesus. Without an authentic expression of the life principles and values of the One we follow, others will never really come to know who Jesus is. I can talk all I like about my family, but the only way people will really get to know them is when they actually meet my family members in person. The way we introduce people to Jesus is by allowing Him to infiltrate and fill our lives to such a degree that others see Him reflected in us.

Incarnational Mission

Ravi Zacharias once posed the question, "How do you reach a generation that listens with its eyes and thinks with its feelings?"[5] I believe the answer to this question is to engage that generation in meaningful relationship that models the principles of biblical love, by valuing each person's perspective on life, actively listening to the heart and the need of the people being reached, and connecting their story and their personal needs to a loving, forgiving, and relational Savior.

Saint Francis of Assisi said, "Preach the gospel at all times and when necessary use words." Mere words are not going to win many people to Jesus. Modeling the principles of the kingdom and the character of Jesus in the context of meaning-ful relationships is the most effective way to communicate the gospel. As we weave our life story with the stories of those we are trying to reach, Jesus, who lives in and through us, will also be woven into their stories.

Jesus did not minister to the world from a distance. He left heaven and became a man, living with those He was called to reach and serve. He has called us to adopt this "incarnational" model, sending us into the world in the same way His Father sent Him.[6] Jesus and the writers of the New Testament con-stantly remind us that to be effective in mission we need to involve ourselves in the lives of those we are trying to reach. Paul explains this incarnational model:

> Though I am free and belong to no man, I make myself a slave to everyone, to win as many as possible. To the Jews I became like a Jew, to win the Jews. To those under the law I became like one under the law (though I myself am not under the law), so as to win those under the law. To those not having the law I became like one not having the law (though I am not free from God's law but am under Christ's law), so as to win those not having the law. To the weak I became weak, to win the weak. I have become all things to all men so that by all possible means I might save some. I do all this for the sake of the gospel, that I may share in its blessings.[7]

I believe in "proclamation evangelism," where the gospel and Word of God is preached in a public environment and peo-ple are called to respond to the claims of Jesus and the Bible. However, outside of the context of the incarnational involve-ment of believers with the people hearing that preaching, the gospel really has little chance of taking root.

At all the youth evangelism events that I have participated in at which young people have responded to a gospel appeal, almost without exception, these young people have been brought to the event by other young people. It is because of an incarnational relationship with Christians that these young people are exposed to Jesus and respond to the gospel. The event is just the "reaping ground," a culmination of an extensive period of incarnational evangelism. It is also in the context of an incarnational relationship that those who respond to an appeal at an event are followed up and discipled.

Rabbit Hole Christians

Any Christian at any age can and should be consciously involved in incarnational mission. However, as we get older and more established in work and family life, we tend to become isolated and insulated from our peer community, and our capacity to engage in peer-to-peer incarnational evangelism is significantly reduced. This means it has to become more deliberate.

Author Jan Johnson describes this phenomenon as "Rabbit Hole Christianity." She explains, "Many believers are 'Rabbit Hole' Christians. In the morning they pop out of their safe Christian homes, hold their breath at work, scurry home to their families, and then off to their Bible studies, and finally end the day praying for the unbelievers they safely avoided all day."[8]

Intentionally or unintentionally, the reality is that as we move beyond our youth into adulthood, we function with a far smaller group of friends and acquaintances, and our circle of influence and peer interaction gradually shrinks. Because of this age-related drift into truncated social interaction, young people are generally better placed than adults to engage in incarnational evangelism. The youth culture lends itself to the incarnational model because young people are incredibly social and deeply involved in each others' lives.

Even though most young people are often ill-equipped to deal with the complex needs of their peers, they still look to their peers to have all their needs met. When I was involved in outreach programs in local schools in Melbourne, the Victorian Education Department conducted a survey to assess the effectiveness of school counselors. They surveyed thousands of students. One of the questions the survey posed was, "Who would you go to first if you had a serious problem?" Over ninety percent of the students said they would go to a friend first, rather than a parent, teacher, or school counselor.

Young people are looking to each other for answers. They trust each other more than anyone else to provide the guidance they need to get through the relational, emotional, and social challenges they face in their daily lives. Bring into this cultural environment a generation of young people who are committed to incarnational evangelism—to living out the gospel and modeling Jesus to their peers—and you will see an enormous harvest of young people brought into the kingdom of God. Without question, one of the most strategic things the church can do to reach the world for Jesus is equip and mobilize young people to reach their peers.

NOTES

1. Matthew 28:18-20

2. George Barna, "Evangelism Is Most Effective Among Kids," *The Barna Update* (October 11, 2004), published by the Barna Group.

3. Matthew 28:19

4. Matthew 5:14-16

5. Ravi Zacharias, in an address at the United Nations' Prayer Breakfast (September 10, 2002).

6. John 20:21

7. 1 Corinthians 9:19-23

8. Jan Johnson, "Escaping the Christian Ghetto," *Moody Monthly* (Nov. 1987), pp. 81-82.

CHAPTER FIVE

LOVING PEOPLE
INTO THE KINGDOM

Early in my ministry I served as a pastor of a local church in the southeastern suburbs of Melbourne, Australia. In response to needs we were encountering through our youth ministry in the local community, the church ended up establishing a shelter for homeless young people. The house we used for the accommodation program was located next door to the church building. The model we adopted for running the home was called the "lead tenant model," which involved young adult Christian leaders living in the house with the homeless youth. The lead tenant would oversee the day-to-day operation of the home: organizing rosters for meals and domestic duties, providing leadership and accountability, and ultimately modeling Christ to the residents.

The program proved to be very successful. The entire church community supported the young people in the home. We were eventually able to expand the program by encouraging other churches in the area to establish new homes utilizing the lead tenant/church community support model we had developed.

As this youth accommodation program developed, we began to earn a reputation with government youth welfare agencies as an effective youth accommodation program that was prepared to take in "difficult" young people. It wasn't long before the Community Services Department of Victoria (CSV) started referring homeless young people to us.

Darren's Story

One day I had a call from the regional CSV Superintendent of youth services, who personally asked me if we could take a young homeless teenager they had in their care. His name was Darren.[1] He was fifteen years old and had already committed many offenses in his short life. He was especially skilled at car theft. Three social workers were on his case, endeavoring to provide support and help Darren resolve his many problems. Over the previous few years, during the short periods that he was not in institutional care, he had not lasted more than three weeks in any of the foster homes or accommodation facilities where he had been placed.

The superintendent explained that Darren's behavior had been so bad over an extended period of time that all the staff in two government youth accommodation centers refused to care for him any longer. In fact, the staff in one of the centers had gone on strike and would not return to work until Darren was removed from their care. I was told that if accommodation could not be found for Darren, the youth welfare department would have no alternative but to place Darren in a juvenile prison.

When we set up the accommodation home, we had clearly stated that if we had room in the home, we would not turn anyone away—even if he or she came with significant behavioral problems. So we agreed to take Darren.

During his first week in the home, Darren broke most of the windows of the house with a BB gun, as well as breaking several windows in the church. Needless to say, after several weeks of this sort of behavior he was eventually asked to leave. However, I made it very clear to him that we wanted him in the home, and if he was prepared to meet a number of criteria for his return, including recompense for the damage he had done, we would readily have him back.

Surprisingly, he wanted to return. Apparently in the short time that he had been with us, he had experienced more genuine care and support than he had ever received in all of his past placements. To the amazement of his social workers, he met all the criteria for his return and managed to move back into the home. However, things did not go smoothly and he caused many more problems for us.

One night in the early hours of the morning, he confronted one of the other residents of the home with a brushcutter.[2] By the time I got to the house, he had the guy trapped in the corner of the kitchen with the brushcutter going full bore, inches from his face. It wasn't hard to diffuse the situation, and Darren was very quick to back down after I arrived. But this was just one of many incidents that almost completely exhausted our patience, grace, and perseverance.

One of Darren's responsibilities in the home was to vacuum the carpet. It wasn't an easy job as the carpet was a long shag pile. So one night Darren brought a lawn mower into the house and endeavored to "mow the carpet." It created a huge mess, with the lawn mower tangled in the pile of the carpet, and impossible to extract without cutting a huge hole in the carpet.

Darren was also a chronic car thief, and many of his convictions were related to his car-stealing activities. One day while visiting the house I noticed five cars in the church parking lot. I knew there was nothing going on in the church and that Darren was the only one home in the accommodation house. So I asked Darren if he knew who the cars belonged to. He casually replied that he and his friends had stolen the cars the previous night. What do you do with five stolen cars in a church parking lot? I told Darren to call his friends and have them come and put the cars back where they came from. The cars were gone by the end of the day.

A Bunch of Keys

A real breakthrough came one Sunday afternoon when I visited Darren in the accommodation home. I brought my four-year-old son, Michael, with me. As soon as we got in the house, Michael ran over to Darren and gave him a big hug. He then proceeded to fish around in Darren's pocket and ended up extracting a bunch of keys, which he played with while I was talking to Darren. When it came time for us to leave, this hardened street kid asked Michael if he wanted the keys. Michael of course was very keen to have them. So Darren ceremoniously handed the keys to Michael and said he could keep them.

We subsequently discovered that this bunch of keys contained the master keys for all the popular makes and models of the cars Darren had been stealing. These keys were Darren's most prized possession. It was the unconditional love and acceptance of a four-year-old boy that finally broke through the hardened exterior of this very damaged and hurting young man.

As I said, it was Sunday afternoon when Darren gave Michael the keys. That evening five of Darren's friends turned up at the house and asked him to go out with them to steal cars. Darren told them that he wasn't going, and although until that moment he had never shown any interest in attending church, he declared to his friends that he was going to church instead of going to steal cars.

Darren had never experienced real family. He had been deserted and abused from the time of his birth. In fact, he had one of the most horrific stories of abuse and rejection I had ever heard. After being deserted by his mother, all the families he had been placed with also rejected him and betrayed his trust. He trusted no one and lived by the laws of the street jungle. When he came into our accommodation home, he found people who cared for him and valued him no matter what he did. But even then he didn't trust this love. Experience had taught him that all those who said that they loved him in the past eventually betrayed him. It wasn't until he encountered the uncomplicated and completely innocent acceptance and love of a four-year-old boy that he finally understood the unconditional love of Jesus. My son looked at Darren and didn't see the rough exterior, or the anger and bad behavior; he saw someone he knew, accepted, valued, and loved for who he was.

Darren eventually gave his life to Jesus. He remained in our accommodation home for another two years. We were able to reconnect him with his father and some of his family members. He got a job and was eventually able to help others in their journey in life.

The following poem was written by another resident in the accommodation home. I share it with you because it captures well the characteristics of unconditional love from the perspective of one receiving it.

Always There

"A tough nut," I heard the copper[3] tell his mate.

Tough? I guess I am, or is it just the hate?

They said next time I'd go to jail.

Again you were there to take me home—pay the bail.

At school they branded me a lazy young punk,

But they hadn't seen my mother, on the floor dead drunk.

And when the church said get lost, you're no use,

They hadn't known my stepfather, the yelling and abuse.

I don't know what possessed you to take me under your wing.

I guess the answer may lie in the moving songs that you sing.

But I am thankful for your open door.

And the time you give to me.

For your patience, jokes, and smile.

You're the first to believe in me for quite a while.

The time I came home drunk, scratched your car
and made you sad.

The time I found you crying 'cuz friends said that
you were mad.

The days you probably needed to be alone.

The weeks I ate you out of house and home.

Camps you took me on, talks on staying at school,

Late night lifts, a birthday party by the pool.

I don't understand why you were so kind.

What was it that you wanted, what did you have in mind?

I made it hard for you, I didn't deserve it, I know.

It cost you greatly when I told you where to go.

Underneath I'm o.k., a little crazy, but I'm real.

I know you see that in me, I know it's how you feel.

But I'm hurting deep inside and I need your loving touch.

I know I've never said it, but I love you so much.

In you I see what's never there in others.

Please never give up on me, or any of the others.

Darren could have been considered one of the "hardest to reach" young people in Australia. Yet even the Darrens of this world can be reached through the application of the unconditional love of Jesus.

The most important Christian attribute we can apply to the task of reaching the world is the love of Jesus. It is the primary fruit of the Spirit that compels us to unconditionally accept and give to others way beyond what is considered reasonable by the world's standards. It is unconditional love that fuels the unique Christian attribute of grace. It is the very thing that defines who we are in Christ and describes who Jesus Christ is to a watching world. And, it is what we need to equip young people with as they venture out as representatives of Jesus and agents of change in a world full of self-interest, conflict, and hatred.

Jesus and the Leper

In Matthew 8:1-4 we read of Jesus' encounter with a leper. As Jesus is coming down from the mountain after delivering his

Sermon on the Mount, he is confronted by a man who has leprosy. The leper throws himself at Jesus' feet and begs to be healed. At the time, Jesus was surrounded by a huge crowd of people who had followed Him down from the mountain. As the leper approached Jesus, I am sure that many in the crowd were horrified. That a leper would come anywhere near them was outrageous. I am also certain that the crowd quickly dispersed to a safe distance, watching and waiting to see how Jesus was going to deal with this unacceptable behavior from an outcast.

Leprosy is a debilitating and alienating disease that, if left untreated, slowly destroys the nervous system. Sensory loss begins in the extremities (toes, fingertips), and as the disease advances, severe injuries occur because cuts, bruises, and even broken bones no longer trigger pain responses in nerves. Opportunistic infections develop that can become gangrenous, causing parts of the body to "die," shrink, and become severely deformed. Eventually the body becomes covered with multiple lesions. Hard nodules and folds of skin form on the face, and the nose may even collapse, giving a person a characteristic lion-like appearance. Blindness also often occurs. A person in an untreated advanced state of leprosy is horribly disfigured. He or she smells of death due to multiple infections and gangrene, and is often viewed by others as a living, rotting corpse.

Throughout history leprosy has been considered as the most despicable of all diseases. Victims have consistently been rejected by their community and kept in separate places such as leper colonies and sanitariums. For example, in Europe during the Middle Ages, people with leprosy were declared dead and were banished after witnessing their own funeral and symbolic burial. Confined to a leprosarium or forced to wander and beg to survive, these outcasts were required to warn others of their presence with a bell or clapper.[4] Even today, most people with leprosy are shunned by their neighbors and are held at arm's length.

It was no different in the time that Jesus walked this earth. If people in the Jewish community were diagnosed with leprosy, they were immediately cast out. They became known as "unclean," and had to leave their family and home and the town they lived in to find whatever habitation they could outside of their local community. They were required to call out, "Unclean!" when anyone came near, to warn them that they were leprous and that they should not be touched. If someone did touch a leper, that person was also declared "unclean" and had to separate himself or herself from the community, and undergo an extensive period of alienation and restoration involving numerous cleansing rituals and requirements. Obviously, people went out of their way to avoid any contact with lepers.

A number of years ago I met a doctor who served with the Leprosy Mission in India. He shared with me his experience when he first started working at the Leprosy Mission's clinic. A man in an advanced stage of leprosy was brought to him for treatment. As this man struggled to get up, the doctor reached out to help him, gently putting his arm around the man to guide him into the examination room. The man immediately started crying. The doctor asked if he was hurting him. "No," the man replied, "you are not hurting me. It's just that no one has touched me in seven years."

This is the context we find in Matthew 8. Here is this leper, standing in front of Jesus, probably grossly disfigured and smelling like a rotting corpse. The crowd has scattered. The people are standing at a safe distance with horrified looks on their faces, wondering why Jesus is allowing a leper to come so close to Him. Jesus intends to heal. But Jesus has more to give this man than physical healing. Jesus could easily just speak a word and the man would be healed. But what does Jesus do? Before He heals the leper, while he is still "unclean," while he is still an "untouchable," Jesus reaches out His hand and touches him. It is only after He touches the leper that Jesus heals him. Jesus knew that more than anything else, this man needed to be loved. By touching the leper before He healed him, Jesus showed the man that He loved him and accepted him, no matter what he looked like or what others thought. Jesus accepted him as he was, with all of his ugliness, disease, stench, pain, and bitterness.

By touching the leper before He healed him, Jesus restored the leper's dignity. Imagine the humiliation, the alienation, and the rejection the leper had suffered since being diagnosed and ostracized. As Jesus approached him, I wonder if the leper was thinking, *No, Jesus, don't come near me. Just heal me and then You can come near. I am unclean, I am unlovable and unacceptable. When I am healed, then I will be worthy, then You can touch me.* But Jesus reached out and touched him, and I am sure there was an overwhelming look of love and acceptance that went with the touch. Most of the healing was accomplished in that touch; the physical healing was secondary.

When my four-year-old son, Michael, reached out and touched Darren, he was being Jesus to this hurting and alienated young man. He loved Darren for who he was, with all of his repugnant behavior, mean demeanor, anger, and bitterness.

For the first time in his life Darren was accepted and loved for who he was, and it melted his heart. It is this uncomplicated and unconditional childlike love that Jesus wants us to extend to the world. This love needs to invade every aspect of our lives and interaction with others, for without love we simply cannot be effective representatives of Jesus or agents of the gospel.

An Antidote for Terrorism?

Young people are being used as cannon fodder by Satan and the terrorist leaders of this world. Who is it that you see blowing themselves up on trains in London, in the streets of Baghdad, and in buses and restaurants in Israel? It is certainly not the terrorist leaders, nor the fundamentalist clerics that lead the quasi-religious sects that preach hate and death. No, it is the young adults and teenagers that these peddlers of hate and violence strap their bombs to.

What is driving these young people to give their lives? What is it that angers the terrorist leaders so much that they would resort to such barbaric and violent acts? What is it that provides enough incentive for someone to feel justified in using young people with so much potential and promise to throw their lives away in such tragic acts of suicidal murder?

Many people are trying to answer these questions. I believe that one of the most insightful analyses of the terrorist mind that I have come across is that offered by Thomas Friedman:

> Talk to young Arabs and Muslims anywhere, and this cognitive dissonance and the word "humiliation" always come up very quickly in conversation. It was revealing that when Mahathir Mohammed made his October 16, 2003, farewell speech as prime minister of Malaysia at an Islamic summit he was hosting in his

country, he built his remarks to his fellow Muslim leaders around the question of why their civilization had become so humiliated—a term he used five times. "I will not enumerate the instances of our humiliation," said Mahathir. "Our only reaction is to become more and more angry. Angry people cannot think properly. There is a feeling of hopelessness among Muslim countries and their people. They feel they can do nothing right . . ."

This humiliation is the key. It has always been my view that terrorism is not spawned by the poverty of money. It is spawned by the poverty of dignity. Humiliation is the most underestimated force in international relationships and in human relations. It is when people or nations are humiliated that they really lash out and engage in extreme violence.[5]

When Jesus encountered the leper, He saw past the external disfigurement and looked into the core of the man's soul. Jesus knew that this man had been stripped of his dignity, that he had suffered intense humiliation and devaluation at the hands of his family and community. He knew that he needed healing of his *internal* disfigurement far more than he needed healing of the *external* ravages of the disease. When Jesus reached out His hand and touched the leper, He was addressing the very same humiliation that twists and distorts the terrorists of this world.

But love does even more than restore dignity. It also provides a platform for meaning and purpose. When people are rescued by the unconditional love of Jesus, they in turn become agents of the very love that rescued them. Love is all about giving to others, and it is as we give that we find meaning, purpose, and enormous personal value. The terrorist driven by humiliation is not only looking to retaliate, he is also looking to make an impact in the world, to be noticed. We find our value in the impact we have on others, either for good or for evil. If our existence makes no difference in the world around us, and no one takes any notice of who we are or what we do, then the message we are receiving is that we are of no value in the world. It gives a terrorist leader an enormous sense of significance when his acts of terror and his name are plastered all over the world's television and print media.

When people rescued by love start to give to others, and then see how the people to whom they give are blessed by their giving, it provides a lasting and affirming sense of meaning and purpose—the meaning and purpose that everyone in this world is searching for. This is why we are told by Jesus that it is far more blessed to give than to receive.[6] As we love others, blessing them by giving to them unconditionally, we experience enormous personal blessing ourselves.

Jesus offers unconditional love and acceptance as the ultimate "antidote" for the loss of dignity and humiliation that drives the terrorist. And He offers the youthful recruit of the terrorist a viable alternative to the twisted logic and purpose that lead so many to waste their lives. Through the ministry of YFC I have seen the unconditional love of Jesus rescue numerous young people from the clutches of fundamentalist and terrorist influence in Asia and the Middle East. The antidote works. The challenge is in how we administer it to those who need it most. How do we access the youth most at risk of terrorist manipulation and recruitment? Surely the only way is to have "agents of love" infiltrate the youth communities that the terrorists prey on, and administer Jesus' love to the young and vulnerable before the terrorists can capture their hearts.

And these agents of love will have to be predominantly Christian young people who already belong to these communities. They are already incarnate in the community and therefore are the only ones who can walk with impunity among those most in need, delivering the antidote. Mobilizing young people to serve and represent Jesus in these communities must be one of the most potent strategies available to us in combating the scourge of terrorism.

Love on the Streets of Manila

When I was serving as the Asia Pacific Area Director for YFC, I made several trips to the Philippines. On one of these trips I visited the street kids' ministry that was run by YFC Philippines, in partnership with a local church in the Cubao district of Manila. Every Saturday morning the church building was opened up for the kids who lived on the streets. They would come for clothing, basic medicines, and probably the only decent meal they would have each week.

Joey was one of the young people who attended the YFC program. He was the leader of one of the biggest street gangs in Cubao. Joey had lived on the street since he was eight years old and had been coming to the YFC program for about three years. When he attended his first program, he had just been released from a police lockup, where he had been held on suspicion of murder. Due to a lack of witnesses who were prepared to testify, the charges were dropped. He was an angry, violent, street-hardened young man, who regularly boasted about the people he had killed on the streets. When Joey saw the influence that this program was having on the members of his gang, he confronted a number of the YFC team members and threatened to kill them. But these committed young Christians treated him as they did all the other street kids—they loved him with God's unconditional love and welcomed him into their community of care. Each time he made a threat the leaders responded with love, explaining that even if he killed them, they would die still loving him, in the same way Jesus loved and forgave those who killed Him. Joey had never encountered this sort of courageous love and unconditional acceptance. The barriers inside him gradually crumbled, and after a number of years he finally gave his life to Jesus.

Becoming a Christian didn't take Joey off the street; instead, it took love onto the streets of Cubao. Joey continued to lead the street gang, but now he was motivated by love instead of hate. He sought to serve his gang members rather than dominate and control them. He was determined to find a way to help the young people in his gang live on the streets without having to steal and fight for their very survival. He set up a group called the "Cubao Barkers." They touted for business for the taxis and Jeepneys[7] that transport people around Manila, receiving a few pesos for their trouble. He produced uniforms (printed T-shirts) for all of his gang members, as well as ID cards. This enterprising business allowed many of the street kids to move away from their crime-filled lives and be able to actually buy food instead of stealing it.

When I met Joey, he stood out in the crowd. He had the biggest smile on his face and just exuded the love of Jesus. When he arrived at the church, he immediately came up to the YFC director who leads the team, put his arm around him, and gave him a huge hug, which told so much of the love of Jesus that no words were needed. Joey had become a regular member of the church, along with many of the other street gang members.

Joey could very easily be viewed as someone who was beyond redemption. Yet he was redeemed. And it was not with clever argument or intellectual debate that Joey was won to the Lord, but with an uncomplicated expression of love and acceptance.

Those who have experienced salvation through a simple application of God's love seem to have a far deeper understanding of the forgiveness and grace of God, and therefore a far greater capacity to love others. Redeemed by an experience of Jesus' love, Joey became an agent of the very love that had redeemed him, and he was able to love many of his fellow street kids into God's kingdom.

If We Have Not Love . . .

In 1 Corinthians 13 we are told that whatever we do for Jesus outside of the context of love is worthless.

> If I speak in the tongues of men and of angels, but have not love, I am only a resounding gong or a clanging cymbal. If I have the gift of prophecy and can fathom all mysteries and all knowledge, and if I have a faith that can move mountains, but have not love, I am nothing. If I give all I possess to the poor and surrender my body to the flames, but have not love, I gain nothing.[8]

Let's suppose that someone in your church was extremely wealthy. One day this man announced that he was going to give away all he possessed to the poor. He proceeded to sell off all of his assets and—along with the fortune in cash he had in the bank—gave away all he had to those in need in the church and in the wider community. How do you think that person would be viewed by the church community? Surely such generosity would mark this man as a model Christian, as someone who was really making a difference in this world, and who was a faithful representative of Jesus. I would expect that the church leadership would publicly laud this man and hold him up as an example of what true Christian service is all about.

But let's say this man was a brutal and hard businessman, who treated his employees very poorly, paid them minimum wages, was ruthless in his dealings with any he encountered in the business world, and who had made his fortune through crushing other businesses and destroying the competition. Further, this man was known for his impatience and volcanic anger, and his interpersonal relationships were a mess because of his unforgiving and controlling spirit. It would certainly look like his motive for giving all his money away was not because he particularly felt compassion for the poor, but because he wanted to store up treasure in heaven and look good in the eyes of his fellow believers. Then, according to what we read in 1 Corinthians 13, because this man's life is not characterized or motivated by love, his generous gesture is worthless in God's kingdom; he gained nothing by giving all he possessed to the poor.

Even if we die as martyrs, courageously declaring our faith with our last breath, it is of no value if we do not have love as the driving force of our lives.

In his second letter to the Corinthians,[9] Paul explains that it is love—as expressed in Jesus' ultimate sacrifice on the cross—that "compels" him to reach and serve others. Paul constantly reminds us in his letters to the early church that sacrificial, unconditional love was the driving force behind all that he did for the kingdom. His service for Jesus was fueled by love.

In John 13[10] Jesus tells us that it is only through our love for one another that others will know that we are His followers. Clearly, without love we cannot be effective disciples of Jesus.

Without Love It Is Impossible to Please God

We read in Hebrews that "without faith it is impossible to please God."[11] However, James points out that faith in and of itself is not enough. Unless faith is accompanied by deeds, it is useless.[12] Love is faith in action. The practical application of love in a Christian's daily life expresses his faith in God and portrays Jesus to the world around him. It follows then, that without this practical expression of faith, without love, it is impossible to please God.

John, in his first epistle, asserts that our love for others is the only conclusive evidence of an authentic love for God, and inversely, that a lack of love for others is clear evidence that a person's faith is not genuine.[13] He states, "If anyone says, 'I love God,' yet hates his brother, he is a liar. For anyone who does not love his brother, whom he has seen, cannot love God, whom he has not seen."[14] Genuine redemption is always expressed in a compelling love for others.

Jesus was once asked by a religious leader: Out of all the commandments in the Bible, which was the greatest commandment? Great question! What is the one commandment that we can observe that will enable us to comply with all that God requires of us? Jesus replied, " 'Love the Lord your God with all your heart and with all your soul and with all your mind.' This is the first and greatest commandment. And the second is like it: 'Love your neighbor as yourself.' All the Law and the Prophets hang on these two commandments."[15] You want to please God? You want to be a true follower of Jesus?

Then simply love God with everything that is you, and self-lessly love all the people in your life.

Jesus declares in the gospel of Matthew that it is by our fruit that we will be known as His followers. The spiritual fruit we are to bear is listed in Galatians 5, and guess which fruit heads the list? Love! And when the three greatest Christian virtues are listed in 1 Corinthians 13, what is the final word on these virtues? "The greatest of these is love."[16] Love gets top billing and should be our first priority.

Love—The Great "Leveler" of God's Kingdom

Dr. Jonathan Sacks, a prominent Jewish leader in Britain, once spoke to a group of government, religious, and community leaders about declining societal values. He stated:

> Imagine that you have total power, and you decide to share it with nine other people. How much do you have left? One tenth of what you began with. Imagine you have a sum of money, and you decide to share it with nine other people. How much do you have left? One tenth of what you began with. Now suppose you have a certain amount of love or friendship or influence or ideals and you decide to share those with nine other people, and you do share them, do you have more or less than you began with? You probably have ten times as much.
>
> It follows immediately from this little exercise in arithmetic that power and wealth will always generate conflict. The more of them I have, the less of them you have, and the more I give you, the less I have.[17]

I believe that at the root of all conflict, oppression, and man-made suffering is the pursuit of three things—money, status, and power. All of these are served up in the world as viable alternatives for love or as means to get love. Money, status, and power are never easily shared, and they are in very limited supply. If the driving ambition of people is to obtain any or all of these three things, then it will only result in dissatisfaction, insatiable appetite, and escalating conflict. But as Sacks points out, there is an alternative to the pathway that leads to conflict, and that is the pathway of love.

It is often said that the great "levelers" of this world are taxes and death. No matter a person's life situation, whether the richest and most privileged individual in the world, or the poorest and most destitute, everyone has to pay taxes and everyone will eventually face death. Death is, of course, the ultimate leveler. Although the rich can sometimes delay death, they cannot cheat it. Rich or poor, famous or unknown, important or insignificant, everyone has to face death; all leave this world completely equal, unable to take any material possession with them.

However, there is another great leveler in this world apart from death and taxes, and that is God's love. In God's kingdom all are declared equal. In Galatians we are told there is "neither Jew nor Greek, slave nor free, male nor female, for we are all one in Christ Jesus."[18]

Love is the currency of God's kingdom. It is the ultimate "renewable resource." The more we give, the more is available to us. Love doesn't depend on what material resources you have at your disposal, or what status you have in this world, or what ethnic group you come from; all have an equal capacity to love. From the poorest of the poor living on the streets of Manila, to the richest person in the world—all have the same reservoir of love to draw upon. From God's perspective, we are truly equal and have equal access to all the resources we require to make a huge difference in this world.

What Does Love Look Like and How Do We Practice It?

When the command to love is given in the New Testament, it is not the Greek verb *phileo* that is used, which expresses friendly affection, but the verb *agapao*, which conveys "action" rather than "emotion." Rather than being an emotional response that derives from a deep feeling of affection, *agape* love is directed by the "will" and can actually be commanded as a "duty."

This is why the great love chapter of the Bible, 1 Corinthians 13, defines *agape* love by a list of actions. It declares that if we are to be authentic followers of Jesus, then we need to be people who are characterized by patience and kindness; who do not envy, and are not boastful or proud; are not rude, or self-seeking, are not easily angered; who keep no record of wrongs and who do not delight in evil, but rejoice with the truth. We need to be people who always protect, always hope, and always persevere.[19]

So how do we love like this? C. S. Lewis addresses this question in his book *Mere Christianity*:

> Do not waste time bothering whether you "love" your neighbor; act as if you did. As soon as we do this we find one of the great secrets. When you are behaving as if you loved someone, you will presently come to love him. If you injure someone you dislike, you will find yourself disliking him more. If you do him a good turn, you will find yourself disliking him less. . . . Whenever we do good to another self, just because it is a self, made (like us) by God, and desiring its own happiness as we desire ours, we shall have learned to love it a little more or, at least, to dislike it a little

less. . . . The difference between a Christian and a worldly man is not that the worldly man has only affections or "likings" and the Christian has only "charity." The worldly man treats certain people kindly because he "likes" them: the Christian, trying to treat every one kindly, finds himself liking more and more people as he goes on—including people he could not even imagined himself liking at the beginning.[20]

Many reading this overview of love are probably saying, "I know all this. None of this is new. I have heard about *agape* love since I started attending Sunday school, and I wish I had a dollar for every time I heard a sermon about the Greatest Commandment." But even though the issue of love has been dealt with so often in the church, people just don't seem to be getting it.

The Key to a Successful Marriage

Marriage is the primary building block of society, the relationship in which the application of mutual, unconditional *agape* love is essential for true success. It would be logical to assume that Christians, who claim to follow the teachings and practices of the Author of *agape* love, should be far better at marriage than those who don't follow Jesus. Yet, in Western nations, particularly in the U.S., marriages are failing within the church at the same rate as outside of the church.[21] In some denominations the divorce rate is higher in the church community than it is in the unchurched community.[22] I believe that a simple application of the elements of love as defined in 1 Corinthians 13 would arrest this spiraling divorce rate among Christians. The problem is that we are just not practicing the principles of *agape* love in our marriages, in our families, or in the larger Christian community.

Recently one of my international leadership team members came into my office clearly distressed. I asked him what the problem was. He shared that he belonged to a men's accountability group that met each week to encourage each other and to keep each other accountable in their walk with Christ. What had upset him was that his group had just spent the whole time they were together trying to convince one of the men in the group not to leave his wife. But the man could not be dissuaded. He told them his wife was simply not meeting his needs anymore and that he had found someone else who could.

In my various leadership roles in the church and in youth ministry, I have had the privilege and challenge of preparing many young couples for marriage. Without exception, during the premarital preparation process, the issue of unrealistic expectations had to be addressed. These couples were entering marriage expecting their partner to meet most—if not all—of their emotional and physical needs, a completely unrealistic expectation that was setting them up for disappointment and relational dysfunction that could eventually lead to marital breakdown.

If I were to ask you the question, "What is the opposite of love?" your likely answer would be "hate." This would be the correct answer if I were referring to *phileo* love, because *phileo* love has to do with emotions. But the Bible proposes that the opposite, or more correctly, the antithesis of *agape* love is "fear." First John 4:18 states: "There is no fear in love. But perfect love drives out fear."

The reason Christian marriages are failing on such a large scale is because couples are operating on a value system that engenders fear rather than love. They enter into the marriage relationship with a focus on "taking" rather than "giving," on "self-gratification" rather than "selflessness." The absence of the values and virtues of *agape* love in a marriage opens the door for fear to take root and eventually control the relationship. Because there is the expectation that individual needs will be met by the marriage partner, as each partner fails to meet the needs of his or her spouse, each becomes more disappointed and disillusioned. Eventually, they will begin to withdraw or hold back the things that meet the needs of their partner, usually in retaliation for not having their own needs met. A power play ensues, with each partner either giving only so they can get something in return, or withholding something so that they can punish their partner for not giving them what they need. The end result of this "need-bartering" is a relationship of fear, where each gives to meet their partner's needs motivated by the fear of not having their own needs met, rather than being driven by a desire to meet their partner's needs. Bartering for need gratification is not a good way to run a marriage.

Love cannot be bought or sold. Love only makes sense when it is freely given with no conditions attached. Consider the words in Song of Songs: "If a man tried to buy love with everything he owned, his offer would be utterly despised."[23]

In a marriage relationship based upon *agape* love, each partner is committed to giving unconditionally. Such a relationship is characterized by patience, kindness, forgiveness, selflessness, and wanting the best for each other. Partners are not focused on having their own needs met, but rather on meeting the needs of their spouse. They give not expecting anything in return. Driven by *agape* love, each partner is constantly trying to outgive the other. A marriage based upon *agape* love cannot fail.

Belief Versus Values

So why is it that Christians are not practicing *agape* love in their marriage relationships? Clearly the church teaches about love, and I would expect that most people in the church believe that love is a key attribute of a Christian. But there is a subtle difference between a *belief* and a *value*. Herein lies the problem—many Christians *believe* in the biblical concept of love, but far less adopt *agape* love as a life-changing *value*.

Let me explain. Let's say we are having a conversation about keeping healthy and fit. I tell you that I believe exercise is good for me, and that I know I need to exercise to remain healthy. I tell you that because of this belief I am going to start a daily exercise program. In a month's time, we meet up, and you ask me how my exercise program is going. "Well," I tell you, "I haven't managed to get myself organized yet, but I will, because I have read even more medical and health reports and I absolutely believe that I need to exercise to keep healthy." But six months later we meet up again, and I tell you—along with a bunch of excuses—that I still haven't started my exercise program. After twelve months we meet again, and when you ask about my commitment to exercise, I explain that I am just too busy to fit in a regular exercise program.

The problem is that even though I believe exercise is good for me, and that I need to exercise to remain healthy, my belief is not a value for me. If exercise were a value, it would become a priority in my life, and the higher the value I gave exercise, the greater place exercise would take in my life.

Many Christians *believe* that practicing *agape* love is essential to a healthy Christian life, but few take love on as a *value*, and even fewer make loving others the highest priority in their life. Yet this is what the Bible teaches—that we cannot function as healthy, authentic Christians without making loving others our highest priority.

The Culture of Entitlement

So what is getting in the way of our loving others? It is the value system by which we live. We live in a "culture of entitlement"—a culture that reinforces the view that an individual's rights are paramount over all others; a culture of self-interest that virtually legislates against *agape* love. How can you serve others if you believe that all others in the world exist to serve you? How can you be generous if you believe that your needs should be met before any others? How can you be patient and sacrificial in a society that demands instant gratification? How can you unconditionally love others if you are always looking for something in return?

For those of us living in societies that are media saturated, we are continually bombarded with advertising from companies trying to sell us things that in most cases we don't even need. These companies spend millions of dollars on research to understand the values of those to whom they are selling, and thus work out the triggers that are going to best sell their products. This is why advertising slogans and bylines provide us with such an accurate expression of the values of a society. With this in mind, let's look at some of the most prominent advertising slogans I have seen over the past few years: "The most important person in the world—is you"; "Because you deserve it"; "It's all about you"; "Pamper yourself"; "Because I'm worth it." Or how about the name of a hair salon that my wife Jenny recently visited: "Me, Me, Me."

In our "me-first" society, the culture of entitlement is a huge obstacle for followers of Jesus to overcome, because loving and giving as the Bible instructs ends up being in conflict with the very culture in which we live. The values espoused in God's Word are all about self-denial; unfortunately our postmodern, materialistic society is not good at self-denial.

Jesus says a lot about self-denial:

♦ "If anyone would come after me, he must deny himself and take up his cross and follow me."[24]

♦ "Whoever wants to become great among you must be your servant, and whoever wants to be first must be slave of all."[25]

♦ "You have heard that it was said, 'Eye for eye, and tooth for tooth.' But I tell you, Do not resist an evil person. If someone strikes you on the right cheek, turn to him the other also. And if someone wants to sue you and take your tunic, let him have your cloak as well. If someone forces you to go one mile, go with him two miles. Give to the one who asks you, and do not turn away from the one who wants to borrow from you."[26]

In Philippians we are told, "Do nothing out of selfish ambition or vain conceit, but in humility consider others better than yourselves."[27]

Rather than my rights over everyone else's, in God's kingdom it is everyone else's rights over mine. In fact, when we become Christians, we hand over the "rights" of our lives to Jesus and take on the role of a servant. As Christians we have no rights. Jesus now holds the title to our lives and can do with us whatever He wills. When we finally understand this and accept it, it is liberating. How can someone infringe on our rights when we have none? How can we be selfish with our time, talents, and treasure when they don't even belong to us?

How Dare You Lose My Luggage!

In my international leadership role I spend a lot of time in airports and on airplanes. When travel is part of your daily life, it soon loses its luster and becomes one of the burdens you bear in the pursuit of your calling and ministry. A few years ago, I had just completed a thirty-hour trip involving a number of flights and airport layovers. After such a long trip the last thing one wants to experience is the loss of one's luggage. I had important meetings to attend the day after my arrival and I desperately needed my baggage to arrive with me, as it contained my clothes for the meeting, as well as some papers I needed for my presentation. So I was not happy when I discovered that the airline had misplaced or misrouted my luggage. I headed off to the service desk to let the airline know exactly what I thought of them and their ineptness at luggage transportation.

I was not alone in my grievance. As I waited in line with other luggage-less people, I was able to hear what the passengers in front of me were saying to the girl at the service desk. They were all visibly angry and were being incredibly rude and loud in communicating their complaints. Even though the girl was doing her best to politely explain the situation, she had to continue to endure abusive and aggressive behavior.

As I watched this girl wither under a constant barrage from angry passengers, I realized that I had come up to the desk with the same attitude as these people in front of me. I may not have been as angry or aggressive as the other passengers, but I certainly came with the same attitude of entitlement. After all, I was important and I needed my luggage to carry out my important job! The airline existed to serve my needs, and this girl had better have some answers, and she had better find my luggage. She existed to serve me!

In that moment of objective reality I realized that this was not how things are in God's kingdom. My rights, my "entitlement" to be served by others, even my "ownership" of the things in my suitcase—all were given to Jesus when I handed over my life to Him. My role in life was not to be served, but to serve. And so when I approached the girl at the desk, the first thing I did was apologize for my fellow passengers' behavior. I then asked her how she was coping with all the abuse and aggression. I told her my luggage was missing but that it was okay. I knew she was doing her best to help locate it and I greatly appreciated her help. I expressed my concern and empathy as best I could. She visibly relaxed, and as we chatted about the challenges of dealing with so many disgruntled passengers, I could see she was very close to tears. She explained to me that something had gone wrong with the baggage handling in the airport I had flown in from and she had been dealing with angry people all day. I thanked her profusely for her service, told her she was doing a great job, and once again apologized on behalf of the other passengers. I walked away from that service desk knowing I had, at least on this occasion, been faithful to Jesus by serving someone in real need.

This may seem like an insignificant incident, but it serves as an example of how our salvation and our commitment to live by the principles of God's kingdom must impact every aspect of our lives if we are to be authentic followers of Jesus. If we don't practice *agape* love in the small episodes of life, we won't know how to do so when the major challenges come. Loving and serving others is the only way we will be able to free ourselves from the tyranny of the culture of entitlement.

Young People and Entitlement

Young people today are often viewed as extremely selfish and insensitive to others' needs. They have the reputation as poster children for the culture of entitlement. But I have consistently found that young Christians are far more easily freed from the bondage of entitlement than those of us who have been Christians for many years. As we get older we progressively climb the ladder of importance, increasing our status in the world and in the church. We also start to accumulate an amazing array of material possessions, getting more and more attached to all that the world has to offer. Hence, giving up everything for Jesus—especially our rights—is often a lot harder for us older, more established Christians than it is for the young, because we are so entrenched in the world and its value system.

Because young people are not so entangled in status and material possessions, when it comes to their rights and entitlements in life, they do not have as much to give up. I'm not saying they aren't instinctively selfish and self-centered. I am claiming that those attitudes are often not as deeply ingrained as they are in us. They are still trying to determine where their allegiances lie in life, whether to themselves or to some higher cause or ideal. So when young people are confronted with the call of Jesus to servanthood and selflessness, they are far more ready to give up the title of their lives, adopt the principles of God's kingdom, and love others as Jesus loves the world.

■ ■ ■ ■ ■ ■

If we are going to win this world for Jesus, then we need to practice selfless, unconditional *agape* love. Loving others is the first and most important step in effective evangelism. However, in our money-, status-, and power-oriented world, it seems we are in short supply when it comes to a collective community of people modeling the principles of the kingdom of God on a large scale. We need someone to lead the charge, to act contrary to the current culture, to live revolutionary lives of self-sacrifice that epitomize Jesus. We need people who have broken free of the culture of entitlement by handing over the rights of their lives to Jesus; people who are fueled by *agape* love. People like this can and will change the world.

However, we cannot just cut this generation adrift and let them "do their thing." Just as we need this generation to lead the way in loving people into the kingdom, they equally need us for protection, nurture, and encouragement. Those of us who have been around for a while have a key role to play in supporting this generation who will change the world. To be able to achieve their God-given potential they need us to stand with them, cheering them on, providing affirmation and solidarity, resourcing their dreams and visions, and protecting them from the cynicism, criticism, and hypocrisy that will destroy their passion and tear away their vision. As they love their peers into the kingdom, this generation desperately needs us to love them.

NOTES

1. Name changed to protect privacy.
2. A weed-whipper with a blade attached for slashing.
3. A policeman.
4. "Leprosy," *Encarta Encyclopedia* (1993–2003).
5. Thomas Friedman, *The World Is Flat* (New York: Farrar, Straus and Giroux, 2005), pp. 399-400.
6. Acts 20:35
7. Small three-wheeled motorized vehicles.
8. 1 Corinthians 13:1-3
9. 2 Corinthians 5:14
10. John 13:34-35
11. Hebrews 11:6
12. James 2:20,26
13. 1 John 4:7-21
14. 1 John 4:20
15. Matthew 22:36-40
16. 1 Corinthians 13:13
17. Jonathan Sacks, from speech titled "Our Nation's Poverty of Hope," given at CCF's "Religion and Welfare" conference (June 22, 2000).
18. Galatians 3:28
19. See 1 Corinthians 13:4-7
20. C. S. Lewis, *Mere Christianity* (London: Harper Collins, 1977), pp. 114-115.
21. George Barna, "Born Again Christians Just As Likely to Divorce As Are Non-Christians," *The Barna Update* (September 2004), published by the Barna Group.
22. Ken Camp, "Baptist Divorce Rate Higher than Average," *The Baptist Standard* (January 12, 2000).
23. Song of Songs 8:7 (NLT)
24. Matthew 16:24
25. Mark 10:43-44
26. Matthew 5:38-42
27. Philippians 2:3

CHAPTER SIX

INVESTING IN
THE NEXT WAVE

Real generosity toward the future
lies in giving all to the present.
Albert Camus

Jesus often presents things in very black-and-white terms. When it comes to what it costs to follow Him, Jesus continually challenges us with an "either/or" option rather than a "both/and." In Matthew 6:24 He tells us, "No one can serve two masters. Either he will hate the one and love the other, or he will be devoted to the one and despise the other. You cannot serve both God and Money."

A classic example of this either/or challenge Jesus puts to those who follow Him is the story of the rich young man found in the gospel of Mark.[1] While Jesus was teaching crowds of followers in Judea, a young man asks what he has to do to attain eternal life. Jesus immediately starts questioning the man about his commitment to following God's commandments. His impressive reply is that he has faithfully kept all the commandments since he was a boy.

Clearly this man had a deep desire to live a holy life that was pleasing to God. And he obviously respected Jesus, dropping to his knees before Him and referring to Him as "good teacher." From any perspective he was a godly and devout person, and Jesus could see his deep and authentic desire to be a true follower. In fact, we read that "Jesus looked at him and loved him."[2]

Jesus obviously longed for this man to enter into a genuine and eternal relationship with Him, but the man had a major hurdle to overcome before he could become a true disciple of Jesus. The challenge Jesus put to him was a tough one: "One thing you lack," he said. "Go, sell everything you have and give to the poor, and you will have treasure in heaven. Then come, follow me." We are told that when this young man heard this, his "face fell," and "he went away sad, because he had great wealth."

Jesus' challenge to this rich young man highlighted his ultimate allegiances and priorities in life. Being a true disciple requires that Christ be number one in your life; anything that has a higher priority has to go.

In Luke 14:33 Jesus states, "Any of you who does not give up everything he has cannot be my disciple." And in Mark 8:34-35 Jesus says, "If anyone would come after me, he must deny himself and take up his cross and follow me. For whoever wants to save his life will lose it, but whoever loses his life for me and for the gospel will save it." Following Jesus costs everything—possessions, family, career, ambitions, wealth—and ultimately, our lives.

If we have truly died so that Christ can live in and through us, then as dead people we no longer have any rights over our time, talent, and treasure. When we become Christians, as self-determining individuals we sign over our lives to Jesus; we die to self and Jesus becomes the owner of everything we possess. He then gives us a new life. One of the first duties He assigns us in this new life is to put us in charge of the things that once used to belong to us. He makes us stewards of all that we formerly owned.

Life Priorities

In determining our life values and priorities, I believe that there is a simple formula that can be applied: How much we are prepared to sacrifice for someone or something is directly proportional to the value we place upon that person or thing.

If we are only prepared to spend a few dollars on something or someone, or on some cause or giving opportunity, then obviously we do not place a very high priority on that thing, person, or cause. If something costs us nothing, then it is usually worth little or nothing to us. However, if we are prepared to pay large sums of money for something, or spend large amounts of time serving someone, or devote much energy and time in working for a cause—particularly if it results in our having to go without something else in our lives—then that thing, person, or cause will have high value to us.

Of course, our lives are the ultimate price we can pay for anything. If we are prepared to give our lives for something or someone, then obviously that something or someone has the highest priority and tops the lists of the values or allegiances by which we live. Most of Jesus' disciples died as martyrs.

It's My Money!

My wife was recently chatting with a group of friends that included a married couple and their sixteen-year-old daughter. They were talking about the summer holidays and this teen's parents shared how their daughter secured a summer job looking after a neighbor's home while they were away on vacation.

In just a few weeks she had earned $160. Someone asked the girl what she was going to do with the money. She replied, "Spend it on clothes, of course!" One of the other adults in the group suggested she put some of the money in the bank. Most of the other adults made suggestions how she could spend her money more responsibly. Eventually in frustration the girl stated, "I earned the money; it is mine. I will spend it on what I want to spend it on, and I am going to spend it all on clothes and jewelry!"

The position taken by this sixteen-year-old girl is absolutely correct from the world's perspective. She indeed had earned the money and had every right to spend it on clothes and jewelry for herself. Without Christ, our primary allegiance is to ourselves, and our decisions are based largely on fulfilling our own desires and needs. However, if we truly hand over the ownership of our lives to Jesus, then all that we possess—time, talent, money, material things—are now His to do with as He pleases. We give up the right to spend what we earn—or to use our possessions—without any reference to a higher authority.

Unfortunately, many Christians don't seem to understand what it means to "give your life to Jesus." They act very much like the sixteen-year-old. They consider everything they possess in life to be theirs, and that they therefore have the right to do with it as they choose. They are certainly prepared to give "some" of "their" time, talent, and treasure to Christ, but only to a degree that it will not cause them any significant change in lifestyle.

Giving Our "Junk" to God

Well-known writer, pastor, and speaker Jamie Buckingham, in his book *The Last Word*, talks about giving our best to God rather than the "junk" that we don't need or want.

It's disturbing that I often wait until a thing is almost beyond repair—or out of control—before I give it to God.

Recently a young missionary family moved into our church. The people provided most of the furnishings for their house. Everything but the refrigerator.

That night at the dinner table I had a generous idea. "Our old refrigerator is on its last legs. Why don't we give it to Paul and Ginny, and buy ourselves a new one—with an automatic icemaker?"

"You mean," my discerning wife smiled, "why not give God our leftovers?"

"Yeah, dad," our teenaged Bonnie chimed in, "I thought God was supposed to get the first fruits—not the rotten apples at the bottom of the barrel."

Unfortunately, I'm like the little kid who took two dimes to church—one for the offering and the other for an ice cream cone. When he dropped one coin down the gutter in front of the church, he said, "Sorry, God, there goes your dime."

We still have our old refrigerator. God's servants have a new one—with an automatic icemaker.[3]

Send It to the Missionaries!

When we served on the mission field at an Aboriginal community in Western Australia, we often received packages of "junk" from churches and individuals—old clothes that could only be used as rags, worn-out shoes, even cartons of broken pieces of cookies. We were told by some of the staff at the mission that they once received a box of used toothbrushes!

Quite often people sent boxes full of junk to the mission without even paying the freight costs. Not knowing what was in these boxes, we had to pay to get them released from the freight depot, and then we ended up throwing out nearly everything that was in the boxes. We wondered if people couldn't be bothered taking their junk to the dump, and decided that it was easier to send it to the missionaries. Not only did they avoid having to make a trip to the dump, but it also made them feel good that they were "giving" to missions.

Giving your junk to God is not a good way to show you love and value Him more than anything in this world. Either these people had no idea what God requires of His followers, or they simply chose to ignore God's command that we are to give our best to Him.

Research conducted in the U.S. and other Western nations regarding giving in the church has shown that in times of financial hardship, one of the first things that people will reduce or cut out of their budget—before making any other sacrifices or adjustments to their lifestyle—is their giving to the church and to other charitable causes.[4] When we consider the implications of this research, what does this say about the value or priority that many in the church place on Christ and their relationship with Him?

If we are only giving God the things that we don't want, or if we are only giving out of our excess, then we are not living by the principle that "God owns everything"; and we are certainly not being responsible stewards.

Investing in God's Kingdom

Being a good steward of God's resources involves not only recognizing that God owns everything, but it also requires that we become diligent and wise investors of the things that God has entrusted to us. We need to be constantly seeking God's guidance as to how He wants us to invest in His kingdom. There is an endless array of possibilities and opportunities available to us when considering our investment options.

The primary thing that will prevent us from investing in God's kingdom is an unhealthy attachment to the things that we formerly owned. The following stories are examples of people who have done well at breaking free of this attachment, and have wisely invested time, talent, and treasure in the kingdom of God.

Investing Time
Tommy

During the time that I served as a pastor, we developed a fairly unique youth program. It involved the youth community of the church having complete ownership and oversight of the church's youth ministry. Although I was ultimately responsible for the youth program and provided consulting and support, the young people were given the freedom to do whatever they believed would provide the greatest opportunity to connect with their friends and most effectively communicate the gospel. This included responsibility for the Sunday evening church service.

Due to the fact that the youth had much freedom and discretion about what happened in the Sunday evening program, we ended up with some very contemporary and innovative services. The music was usually loud and the messages very intense and interactive. Mistakes were made, but overall, the services were relevant and effective, attracting many unchurched young people, many of whom made commitments to Christ.

One of the elders of the church was a man named Tommy. Tommy came from a very conservative church background.

Although he had mellowed over the years, he was still well grounded in his conservative heritage.

Every Sunday evening Tommy attended the youth service. However, the first thing he did when he walked through the door was to conspicuously take out some earplugs and shove them into his ears. He then proceeded into the church and sat in the very last seat at the back of the meeting area. Throughout the service Tommy sat there with a stoic and pained expression on his face. Following the service, he departed the building quickly without saying much to anyone and without connecting with the young people.

It wasn't long before one of the young people at a youth ministry leadership meeting asked me why Tommy even bothered to come to the youth service. They had all seen him putting the ear plugs in his ears and noticed how unhappy he seemed to be with what was going on in the service. The leadership team requested that I speak to Tommy about their concerns.

The next Sunday—with some trepidation—I approached Tommy to talk about his attendance at the youth service. I realized that Tommy came from a background where attendance at all church activities and services was expected. I told him that it was obvious that he didn't like the music or the style of the program. I explained to him that this service was solely dedicated to the youth and that he wasn't expected or required to attend.

Tommy's response surprised me. He explained that he certainly didn't like the "loud" music, particularly the drums. He also said he felt "uncomfortable" with much of the content of the service. But he knew God was at work in the youth community and he wanted to be where young people were being reached and were giving their lives to Jesus. He was thrilled with how many young people had become disciples of Jesus through this youth service, and his motivation for attending the service was to support the youth ministry. He said he came to pray. He wanted to participate, and the only way he knew how was to pray. So he came every Sunday evening and sat at the back of the church praying for those leading the youth ministry and for each of the young people attending the service.

When I reported back to the leadership team why Tommy attended the services, their attitude toward Tommy completely turned around. Over the next few weeks I noticed a number of the youth ministry leaders talking to Tommy after the Sunday evening service. The young people started to accept Tommy as part of their community and included him as much as they could in what they were doing. They would share prayer items with him, and he started inviting them to his home for meals. The relationship grew, and Tommy eventually became one of the strongest advocates and supporters of the youth ministry in the church.

Tommy was a good steward of his time. With regards to expertise, funds, experience, and talent, Tommy knew that he had little to offer the youth community of the church. Yet he still found a way to invest in this vital ministry. By investing time and prayer into the youth ministry, he was able to participate in growing the kingdom of God and in reaching young people for Jesus. He could have easily used his time in other activities that would have better served his own needs and comfort, and perpetuated his familiar lifestyle. Attending the youth service was costly—it took Tommy out of his comfort zone—but it was a good use of the resource of time and energy that Tommy had been given by God to invest in His kingdom.

Geoff and Eileen

When I was running big youth events at a convention center in the mountains southeast of Melbourne, Australia, I encountered an older retired couple. They had even less capacity than Tommy to engage in youth ministry, but they had a distinct calling to serve and support youth. Their names were Geoff and Eileen.

We held the main programs of the youth festivals in an open-sided building that seated around three thousand people inside the auditorium, and about another one thousand outside on the grass areas at each side of the building. At every program during one of the weekend festivals, I noticed an older couple sitting on the outside seats farthest away from the stage area. When you have around four thousand young people at a youth event, a couple of "senior citizens" sitting among them are very conspicuous.

Eventually I approached the couple and asked them why they were there. They told me that for many years they had been financial supporters of the Youth for Christ ministry, but now as a retired couple, they no longer had the same capacity to contribute financially. However, they realized they did have one thing in abundance that they could give, and that was time; and one of the best ways to invest that time was to pray. And so they were attending the youth event so they could pray for the crowds of young people as they were exposed to the gospel.

Geoff and Eileen could have easily sat at home relaxing and enjoying their retirement. But they wanted to be more involved. They felt they needed to deliberately and sacrificially enter into the spiritual battle for the lives of young people, and they saw no better way to do this than to be with these young people as they were exposed to the gospel, contending for their lives through prayer. I believe many young people are now members of God's kingdom due to the faithful stewardship of Geoff and Eileen.

We need to see our time as one of the most valuable resources we have available to invest on God's behalf in establishing His kingdom on earth. We can use our time to pray, to encourage others, to serve in the church, to minister to those in need, or to serve our family. There are countless opportunities and options available to us. Consequently, we need to be careful how much we allow the busyness of life to consume this precious resource.

Many people fill up their time with countless activities and commitments, leaving very little "discretionary" time remaining to respond to the opportunities that God brings their way. Work commitments in particular can consume much of our energy and time, leaving us with little remaining to give to others. When deciding on a career path or a job opportunity, we need to remember that all of our time and energy belongs to God, and we need to check with Him about whether pursuing a particular job or career is the best use of our time.

A Sacrificial Sri Lankan Young Leader

A few years ago, during a visit to Sri Lanka, I was chatting with some of the key volunteer leaders working in the YFC ministry. One girl in particular stood out as an exceptionally bright and capable young woman. I asked her if she was considering giving up her career and coming to work full time for YFC. Her reply was both challenging and enlightening. She explained that she already considered that she was working full time for God in the YFC ministry. Her job was just a way for her to sustain herself and to "fund" her ministry. In fact, she told me that she had just been offered a promotion to a senior role in the firm where she worked. But she turned down the offer and was now looking for a less demanding position—with far less pay and prospects for advancement—so that she could free up more time to serve Jesus in YFC.

This young Sri Lankan leader had the right perspective on the use of her time. As a follower of Jesus, her priority was serving Him and investing her time, talent, and treasure in His work. She was prepared to make life choices based not on what would make her life more comfortable, or improve her career prospects, but on what would provide her with the greatest opportunity to serve Jesus and to share His love and grace with others.

I am not suggesting that every Christian needs to give up a career so he or she can free up time to serve God. Nor am I suggesting that we should consider the time we spend at work as "unproductive time" that must be deleted from the time we have available to allocate to God. The people with whom we work need Jesus as much as anyone else. We can legitimately view our place of employment as the mission field where God has placed us. But we need to remember that our primary criteria for deciding what career path we take, or what employment we pursue, must be whether it is the best use of our time in growing the kingdom of God.

Many people work excessive hours so that they can fund a lifestyle that they believe is necessary for happiness. Their motivation for working is to achieve certain material goals, and the use of their time is largely directed to meeting the demands of their material desires and dreams. If we are completely consumed by our career so that we have no time left for God—for prayer, for Christian service, for study of God's Word, for caring for our family, for sharing our faith with others, and serving those in need—then we are not being good stewards of our time.

Time is a valuable but finite resource that is being expended every moment we spend on this planet. Let's make sure we spend it wisely in the service of Jesus.

Investing Talent
Growing Cows for Jesus

For a community of farmers living in Park River, North Dakota, the fact that they had no money to give to missions didn't prevent them from finding a way to fund mission projects. In 1957 a revival swept through this small farming community. Many farming families were challenged to invest in God's kingdom, especially in mission initiatives that were taking the gospel to unreached people all over the world.

These farmers realized that although they had very little funds to give to missions, they did have something they could give, and that was their experience and expertise in farming. They knew how to grow cattle. And so with the help of the Reverend Ed Folden, a local pastor, they raised enough funds from local businesses to buy some calves. Each farmer was allocated one or two of these calves. The farmers were responsible for growing these calves to maturity. They would then be sold at market and the proceeds given to missions. I am sure that the farmers gave these cattle the best of care as they ran with the rest of the herd, knowing that these were "God's cows."

When the mature cattle were sold, enough of the proceeds

of the sale were held back to purchase another calf, allowing the original donated funds to be used over and over again. The remainder of the cattle sale funds was given to missions. This process allowed even the poorest farming family to be involved in giving to missions through the investment of their farming "talent."

This concept worked so well that the Reverend Folden shared the idea with other farming communities. Eventually he formed an organization called Steer Inc. Since 1957, well over $12 million has been given to missions through Steer Inc.

Investing Vocational Skills in the Kingdom
We are told in Colossians 3:23, "Whatever you do, work at it with all your heart, as working for the Lord, not for men." There are endless opportunities for God's people to invest career skills and business acumen in mission and service, applying their talents to resourcing and supporting missions and ministry. Vocation, education, experience, training, talent—all can be invested in God's kingdom.

When I heard the story of Steer Inc., it captivated my imagination. I realized that this concept of investing skills and vocational capability in God's kingdom had a far broader application than the farming community. I decided I would share the concept with some friends who were successful business owners and see how they reacted.

I arranged to meet with a good friend who had a very successful business and was a committed and generous supporter of our ministry. His area of expertise was medical insurance and retirement plans. I told him the Steer story, and then explored with him whether he thought this concept could be applied in his business and vocational context.

As he explained his business to me—how it involved managing a large company's employee medical insurance and retirement plans—I had an idea. I suggested that he select a new account that he was planning to bid for, and that he dedicate this account to missions. If he won the bid, then this would become "God's account," and all the proceeds would be directed to supporting ministry and missions. In this way he would be able to invest his unique talents and expertise in growing God's kingdom.

He was very positive about the suggestion and said he could already think of an account he could "bid on" for God. If he won the account, it would generate regular commissions and fees and continue to fund missions for many years, as the commissions on large accounts such as this were substantial.

When we got together again a couple of weeks later, he was effusive about this opportunity to invest his skills and talents in God's kingdom. He shared with me how over the past few years he had lost his passion for his business, explaining that when he started in business many years ago, everything was new and challenging and he was very energized by what he was doing. But now he had everything he required to live a very comfortable life and didn't need to grow his business any further. He was just going through the motions of maintaining his business.

But this opportunity to bid on an account for God reenergized him. He desperately wanted to win this account for the kingdom and he was applying all his skills, experience, and talent to the task. This kingdom investment concept brought new purpose and motivation to his life and business. It validated his business acumen and skills as legitimate in the service of God and as needed and worthy tools for growing God's kingdom.

I was encouraged by this experience and started sharing the concept with others. Everyone I shared it with responded positively. A man who builds condominiums allocated the profit from every twentieth condo he built to missions. A shopping center developer dedicated one of the shops in a new development to God, with the view that it would generate ongoing income for the kingdom. Each person I talked to was excited about the opportunity to utilize his or her skills and talents to invest in missions and ministry.

Builders Without Borders

Another great example of people investing their talent in the kingdom came about as a result of a visit by Jean Baptiste Mugarura—the national director of YFC Rwanda—to Fort Myers, Florida. Jean Baptiste was trying to raise money to purchase some land in Kigali. His long-term vision was to build a youth training center and school to educate, train, and equip young leaders. The land purchase was the first challenge Jean Baptiste needed to overcome to see his vision become a reality.

He heard of a man who owned a home construction company in Fort Myers who might be able to help with a financial contribution for the land purchase, so he arranged to meet with this man, whose name was Dan. After Jean Baptiste shared his story, Dan was moved and prompted by God to give a generous financial donation. When Jean Baptiste asked Dan if he knew anyone else who may be interested in his ministry, Dan introduced him to Lanny, another businessman involved in the building industry who owned a very successful local building material supply company. Lanny was also touched by Jean Baptiste's story and made a generous donation, which, along with Dan's gift, was enough for Jean Baptiste to purchase the land.

However, the story doesn't end there. Jean Baptiste returned to Fort Myers a year later to report to Dan and Lanny what he had done with the money they had given. He also shared with them the vision he had for the development of a training center and school for training young leaders who would be sent out to evangelize and serve young people not only in Rwanda, but throughout East Africa. As Jean Baptiste shared his vision these practical businesspeople—who up until this moment in time had believed that the main contribution they could make to missions was through giving money—started to catch their own vision. They realized that not only could they use their business skills to generate the money needed for this project, they could also use their expertise in construction and building design to help build the training center.

They told Jean Baptiste that they would build the training center for him. They then set about designing a building the size and configuration required for the training center. They obtained the building materials, prefabricated the building in Florida, packed the building in two huge shipping containers, transported the building to Rwanda, recruited a team of builders and tradespeople, traveled to Rwanda with the team, and in three weeks built a training center large enough to house and train five hundred young leaders.

After this initial experience of using their talents to engage in mission, Lanny and Dan undertook several other projects in Rwanda, recruiting more teams of builders and skilled tradespeople. In two years they were able to build a whole school comprised of five huge buildings containing classrooms to accommodate six hundred students, the school administration offices, a computer lab, science rooms, a library, and bathroom facilities. They went on to set up an organization called Builders Without Borders and, along with some other very committed and talented people, are now involved in mobilizing many others in the building industry to invest their gifts and talents in strategic mission projects across the world.

Many people believe, and are often told, that if they truly want to serve God, they need to give up their career and go to the mission field. But this is not what God requires. Sure, some are called to "full-time" missionary service on the traditional "mission field." But others are called to full-time missionary service in business, or in education, or in the service industry.

We are called to be "full-time missionaries" wherever God places us. God has uniquely gifted many of His followers with particular business and vocational skills, and I believe He desires that all His followers invest these skills where they can best be used by Him. I don't have a clue how to sell insurance and retirement plans to big companies, but my friend does. And selling insurance to resource and grow the kingdom of God is just as legitimate a calling as mine is to serve in a worldwide youth ministry. And further, people in the marketplace have access to many who desperately need the love of Christ and yet are far outside the circle of influence of the church and other Christians. Their mission field comprises the people they connect with in the marketplace.

Whatever gifts, talents, skills, and expertise we possess, God can use them to grow and resource His kingdom. God has uniquely gifted every member of His family so he or she can be light and salt in the world. Utilizing our gifts and talents to serve God in our vocational context is a vital part of our stewardship responsibility.

Investing Treasure

When I started out in my role as area director for YFC Asia Pacific, we had some significant financial needs. We were implementing a major mission strategy, and I was somewhat overwhelmed by the challenges of resourcing such an ambitious and visionary plan.

For a number of years I had been supported in my various leadership roles by a couple who have a very healthy attitude when it comes to ownership of their earthly treasure. Through a letter I had sent out to our supporters sharing about our mission plans, this couple became aware of our pressing need for finances. They telephoned me to ask how much we required to cover the need. I responded with what I thought was a pretty bold request, stating, "Ten thousand dollars would really help." They replied that this was not what they had asked; they wanted to know what the real need was. So I told them that we actually needed $22,000. They immediately responded that they would transfer $22,000 to our account that very day.

I was thrilled that this couple was prepared to provide all the funds we needed and effusively thanked them for their generosity. However, I still had a valuable lesson to learn. The couple went on to share with me that before they called me, they had prayed about what they should give and had written down a figure on a piece of paper. The figure that God had given them, of course, was $22,000. They told me in the future to always honestly share the real need, and allow God to decide whether they were the ones who should meet that need. I had made the mistake of initially deciding for them what would be a reasonable amount for them to give, instead of trusting God to speak to them about what He would have them give in response to the need.

However, the story doesn't end there. I subsequently discovered that for some time this couple had been saving to purchase a new car. The one they were driving was over ten years old and had many miles on it. It was the money they had saved to replace their old car that they had given to meet the need I had shared with them.

About a year after this generous and sacrificial act of giving, I once again presented this couple with a financial need. This time I had learned my lesson and I told them exactly what we required. It was a substantial sum, significantly more than the $22,000 they had given the previous year. They said they would pray about it and get back to me. A few weeks later they transferred the whole amount we needed to our bank account. It wasn't until a year or so after this that I found out that they had extended the mortgage on their home to cover this large donation.

This couple knew what it means to be good stewards of God's resources. Everything they possessed belonged to God, and whenever He made it clear to them that He required some of these resources, they would give freely and cheerfully. I know of very few people who have such a loose attachment to their possessions and money as this couple does; but this is how God asks us to live. If He requires something that we consider to be ours—money, house, car—no matter what it is, it is His to take and use for His purposes.

The Parable of the Talents
In Jesus' parable about the talents, found in Matthew 25:14-30, He instructs us—as His servants—to make good use of

all He has given us. Jesus tells the story of a man who, before leaving on a long journey, entrusted various amounts of money to three of his servants, with the expectation that they invest this money and achieve a return on the investment for their master. Two of the servants immediately put the money to work, wisely investing the funds and attaining good returns. The third servant was afraid to take any risks with his master's money, so he dug a hole in the ground and hid the money until his master returned.

When the master finally returned from the long journey, he asked each of his servants to report on what they had done with the money he had entrusted to them. He was very pleased with the reports of the first two servants, who astutely invested the money and achieved good returns on their investments. He commended them for their faithful service, celebrated their achievements with them, and gave them additional responsibilities in his kingdom. However, when the third servant reported to him that he had been afraid that he would lose the money and therefore had done nothing with it during his master's absence, the master was furious with him. He told him that he could at least have put the money in the bank and earned some interest. The master took back the money and gave it to one of the other servants who had been faithful. Then he declared, "To those who use well what they are given, even more will be given, and they will have an abundance. But from those who are unfaithful, even what little they have will be taken away. Now throw this useless servant into outer darkness, where there will be weeping and gnashing of teeth."[5]

The context of this parable was Jesus' teaching on the final judgment of the world. Clearly what Jesus is conveying to His followers through this story is that we will all have to give an account to Him for what we have done with the resources He has entrusted to us. In 1 Corinthians 3:13 (NLT) we are told, "There is going to come a time of testing at the judgment day to see what kind of work each builder has done. Everyone's work will be put through the fire to see whether or not it keeps its value."

As Christians we are subservient to Christ. Jesus is our Master and we are His servants. We will all have to give account for what we have done with the time, talent, and treasure that He has entrusted to us to invest in this world on His behalf. How many of us are going to end up reporting to Jesus that we spent most or all of His resources on ourselves? Or that we really didn't have a clue what to do with what He had given us, and so we just used it up on other things not of the kingdom?

Or are we going to be able to report to Jesus that we invested His resources wisely, and present Him with a good return on His investment. Are we going to be able to say, "I made good use of what You gave me, Lord. Here are the people I am bringing with me into the kingdom. And over there are the people I resourced and served and encouraged, and look at how productive they have been. Lord, look at all those they are bringing into the kingdom with them."

Will our Lord and Master commend us in the same way He commended the faithful servants in the parable of the talents? Will He say to us, "Well done, my good and faithful servant. You have been faithful in handling this small amount, so now I will give you many more responsibilities. Let's celebrate together"?[6]

The opportunities to invest what Jesus has entrusted to us are numerous. One of the most exciting investment opportunities available is in resourcing, supporting, encouraging, mentoring, and serving this current generation of young people who are going to be at the forefront of the next wave of mission. Investing our time, talent, and treasure in this "next wave" generation will maximize their impact on the world. Can you imagine the joy of standing before Jesus alongside these world-changing young leaders, and together presenting to Jesus the product of our investments? Of being able to say to Jesus, "Look, Lord, I took what You entrusted to me and I invested it in these young leaders, and here is the result of my investment—a multitude of Your followers from every corner of the world." I think Jesus would be pleased and would have great cause to celebrate with us.

NOTES

1. Mark 10:17-31

2. Mark 10:21

3. Jamie Buckingham, *The Last Word* (Plainfield, NJ: Logos International, 1978), pp. 86-87.

4. See *Giving and Volunteering in the United States* (Washington, DC: Independent Sector, 2001).

5. Matthew 25:29-30 (NLT)

6. Matthew 25:23 (NLT)

CHAPTER SEVEN

MENTORING
THE NEXT WAVE

For four years my wife, Jenny, and I lived in an Aboriginal community at the edge of the desert in Western Australia, just outside the gold mining town of Kalgoorlie. It was our first mission experience. The main ministry of the mission was caring for neglected, abused, and abandoned Aboriginal children.

During the school holidays we would pile all the kids into a couple of buses and drive 250 miles to the town of Esperence, where we had a holiday camp owned by the mission. Esperence is a remote coastal town with pristine beaches, crystal clear water, and beautiful scenery. The kids loved the place, and we spent most of our time on the beach swimming and surfing.

One of my favorite pastimes is fishing. When I was growing up, my family regularly vacationed at the beach, and once I could hold a fishing pole I spent countless hours fishing off the rocks, beaches, or jetties. I figured that the Aboriginal kids would enjoy fishing as much as I did, so on the first trip I made to Esperence, I organized a fishing expedition to the local jetty.

Before taking the kids fishing, I was wise enough to ask the lady who ran the campsite for her fishing secrets. She was a renowned fisherwoman with a legendary ability to catch fish on the local jetty, even when no one else was catching anything. She told me that the easiest fish to catch were herring, and that you didn't need any fancy gear to catch them, only a very light hand-line with no weight. The bait she recommended was ground beef. She explained how you needed to place a little of the ground meat on the end of a small hook, dip it into pollard—a powdery derivative of wheat used to feed chickens—and then simply lower it into the water and let it drift, occasionally giving it a little tug to disperse the pollard.

As I was heading down to the jetty with about thirty Aboriginal kids in tow and a bucket of pollard, a bag of ground beef, and a bunch of hand-lines, I must admit that I was thinking, *This is not going to work.* I had been a keen fisherman for years and had never heard of using ground beef and chicken feed for bait! And these kids, born and raised in the bush, didn't have a clue when it came to fishing. I thought, *Well, we'll just drop the lines in for a while and when the kids get bored, we'll go down to the beach for a swim.*

As we made our way onto the jetty we passed a few people who were fishing. I asked them whether they had caught anything. The reply was not encouraging; none of them had caught even one fish, and some had been fishing for a couple of hours.

I lined up the kids along the jetty, handed out the hand-lines, and explained how to bait the hook and dip it in the pollard. Then I set myself up and dropped in my line. In less than a few minutes I had a nice-sized herring on the hook and was struggling to get it onto the jetty. After that, it just went crazy.

The kids started catching fish all along the jetty. The problem was that they would pull up a fish and have no idea what to do with it. They usually ended up dropping it onto the jetty in the middle of their hand-line, and it would flip all over the place tangling up the line, with the kids yelling for me to help them. I found myself running up and down the jetty, trying to get the fish free from the tangled line, off the hook, and in the bucket. I then had to untangle the pile of line the fish had been flapping around in, rebait the hook, and get it back in the water.

In a little more than an hour, we had caught 150 fish! The only problem was that in all the time we had been at the jetty, I had only fished for a couple of minutes. So I only caught one fish! But I was suddenly surrounded with brand-new enthusiastic fishermen! We went fishing again, of course, and each time we caught enough fish to feed all the people we had at the camp.

Young people are quick learners. The more we went fishing, the more the kids improved in their fishing technique. Even though I was still busy helping them bait their hooks, remove their fish, and untangle their lines, I was eventually freed up enough to catch a few fish myself, allowing me to be even more effective in teaching the Aboriginal kids how to fish, as I was able to also model how it was done.

Mentoring Disciples

As followers of Jesus we are called to make disciples. In any evangelism process we must always keep in mind that our task is not simply to get people to make a commitment to Jesus; it is to make lifelong disciples of Jesus who follow and practice His teachings and lifestyle.

My fishing story serves as an example of the value of mentoring. I don't think we would have caught many fish if I had only concentrated on catching fish myself and had left the Aboriginal kids to fend for themselves. Teaching, supporting, encouraging, and modeling is what mentoring is all about. I was able to multiply my fishing effectiveness thirtyfold through a simple process of mentoring.

I believe that mentoring is the key to making authentic disciples of Jesus. Empowering and equipping an emerging global generation of young disciples through a process of ongoing mentoring will be like throwing fuel on a fire. Mentoring will significantly multiply their effectiveness. We cannot overestimate the value of mentoring when it comes to the development of young disciples of Jesus.

Jesus says, "Come, follow me, and I will make you fishers of men."[1] Many people respond to Jesus' call but fail to ever develop into effective "fishers of men." Just as the Aboriginal kids got into all kinds of trouble when they first attempted fishing, so new believers in Christ will very soon encounter the tangles that can occur when they get out there "fishing" for Jesus. They need mentors to stand with them, encouraging them and helping them to untangle their lives as they get enmeshed with the complexities of living for Jesus in a fallen world.

One significant role that a mentor plays in the life of young Christians is protecting them from the ravages of hypocrisy and soul-destroying criticism. Hypocrisy very quickly undermines the simple, innocent faith of a new believer, causing disillusionment and blurring of the character of Christ. And nothing quenches the fire of enthusiasm and vision in a young Christian faster than a good dose of unhelpful criticism.

Criticism and Hypocrisy

When I was a teenager growing up in a conservative church in the northern suburbs of Melbourne, I was deeply hurt and discouraged by an incident that occurred in a meeting between the leadership of the church and a group of young people. The youth group leaders had arranged a meeting with the church eldership to allow a number of us to present our concerns to the elders. There was a rising level of discontent in the youth community over the lack of cultural relevance of the church to our peers, and some of us in the youth group were advocating for change so that we could more effectively reach our friends and integrate them into the church.

At the meeting we were given the opportunity to put our case to the elders. One of my closest friends spoke up first. In trying to explain the challenges we were facing in bridging the cultural divide, my friend stated that he would be "embarrassed" to bring one of his unchurched friends to an outreach service, because the services were so conservative and alien to the youth culture in which he lived. Before he could say any more, one of the elders jumped to his feet and in an angry voice, and with an accusing finger pointed at my friend, stated, "How dare you say you are ashamed of your faith." He then quoted Mark 8:38 (KJV), which says, "Whosoever therefore shall be ashamed of me and of my words in this adulterous and sinful generation; of him also shall the Son of man be ashamed, when he cometh in the glory of his Father with the holy angels." He proceeded with a barrage of criticism of youth in general, lecturing us all on what he saw as a weakness of faith that had resulted in us "selling out" to the world and compromising our witness by trying to incorporate the world's corrupt culture into the church.

I watched as my friend visibly wilted under this barrage of unwarranted and vitriolic criticism. This elder had completely misunderstood what my friend was saying. Blinded by his own self-righteousness, he was unable to see the passion and love that this young man had for his lost friends. His insensitivity, critical spirit, and blatant hypocrisy resulted in my friend's innocent and simple faith being severely shaken.

Young Christians do not cope well with critical hypocrisy. My friend was not only humiliated and discouraged by the hurtful criticism, but he was also completely disillusioned by the hypocrisy of this so-called Christian leader who claimed to love and represent Jesus, but expressed only legalism and self-righteous indignation. The hallmarks of authentic and godly leadership—love, joy, peace, patience, kindness, goodness, faithfulness, gentleness, and self-control[2]—were glaringly absent in this church leader's response to this young Christian's genuine and impassioned plea for authenticity and relevance.

If we fill the role of a Christian leader, yet do not portray or live by the values and characteristics of Christ, we are walking on very dangerous ground. Jesus clearly viewed the hypocrisy of spiritual leaders as one of the most dangerous things faced by a new believer. He harshly condemned the Pharisees for their hypocrisy. Here is just a small sample of what our Lord had to say about these Jewish religious leaders who claimed to represent God: "The teachers of the law and the Pharisees sit in Moses' seat. So you must obey them and do everything they tell you. But do not do what they do, for they do not practice what they preach."[3] Jesus confronted their twisted efforts to recruit others: "Woe to you, teachers of the law and Pharisees, you hypocrites! You travel over land and sea to win a single convert, and when he becomes one, you make him twice as much a son of hell as you are."[4] And He warned them of their inconsistent lives: "Woe to you, teachers of the law and Pharisees, you hypocrites! You are like whitewashed tombs, which look beautiful on the outside but on the inside are full of dead men's bones and everything unclean. In the same way, on the outside you appear to people as righteous but on the inside you are full of hypocrisy and wickedness."[5]

Any leadership role in the church comes with an enormous amount of responsibility. Effective leadership resides not in how well we organize ourselves or others, or in how many people we attract to the church, or even in how well we motivate people through our oratory skills and charisma. Godly leadership is seen far more in how we model and represent Jesus to those we lead. Leadership in God's kingdom is all about character and authenticity. And when it comes to leading and caring for vulnerable and impressionable young believers, let's consider carefully the words of Jesus in Matthew: "But if anyone causes one of these little ones who believe in me to sin, it would be better for him to have a large millstone hung around his neck and to be drowned in the depths of the sea."[6]

What my young friend needed most at this vulnerable and fragile point of his Christian walk was an authentic and godly mentor. He needed someone to defend him and to advocate for him, to jump in and fight on his behalf. He needed someone to nurture him, pray with him, and care for him after he had been wounded by the attack at the meeting. He needed someone to explain to him why Christians are so often very poor representatives of Jesus. He needed someone to be Jesus to him, to love him with the love of Christ, and to walk with him through the valley of betrayal and bitterness. But my friend didn't have a mentor, and I only served in my anger and immaturity to reinforce his bitterness and cynicism.

After the elder had delivered his lecture at this meeting, none of the other young people was game enough to speak. The meeting deteriorated into a one-sided affair, with the youth leaders making no progress at all in brokering change. The status quo was maintained and the church continued to be culturally irrelevant to young people. My friend became more and more cynical about his faith and other Christians. He slowly drifted away from the church and ceased to even identify himself as a Christian among his friends.

Although I remained at the church, I was discouraged and bitter. I became disruptive and unhelpful in the youth group. I started drifting in my faith and lost any enthusiasm I had for church. I was on my way out. The only reason I remained was because my whole family attended the church, so I just kept attending with them.

Prayer Mentoring

I am not sure where I would be today if it were not for the intervention of a "prayer mentor." One Sunday morning, while I was standing in the church foyer with a group of friends, an older man came up to me, put his hand on my shoulder, and simply said, "I just want you to know that I pray for you every day." Then without saying anything more, he walked away. I only vaguely knew this man. His name was Will Cavill, and he had been in the church for years. He was a quiet, gentle man who, as far as I knew, didn't have any significant role in the church.

I left the church that day disturbed. I couldn't stop thinking about what Mr. Cavill had said to me. Why would he pray for me every day? I thought maybe he told *everyone* he was praying for them. So I asked my friends whether Mr. Cavill had told them he was praying for them as well. I soon discovered that he had not spoken to any of my friends, and it seemed from asking around that he had also not approached anyone else in the youth community. A couple of weeks later Mr. Cavill once more told me he was praying for me, but this time I didn't let him get away without first asking him why he was praying for me. He said that he believed God had something special in store for me, and that the Lord had laid me on his heart, and so he was praying for me every day.

A few months after first telling me that he was praying for me, Mr. Cavill asked me to attend a church prayer meeting with him. The last thing I wanted to do was go to a prayer meeting populated with a bunch of "old" people, including the elder who had attacked my friend. But how could I say no to a guy who prayed for me every day? So off I went to the prayer meeting. From then on, every time Mr. Cavill asked me to attend the prayer meeting, I went with him.

One day before going into the prayer meeting, Mr. Cavill encouraged me to pray in the meeting. In the middle of the meeting I offered up a very tentative and halting prayer. Afterward Mr. Cavill and a number of the other people in the meeting went out of their way to encourage and affirm me. From that day on I started to care a whole lot more about what was happening in the church. I got more engaged in the youth group and church activities. I eventually was baptized (our church practiced full-immersion baptism) and I started to develop a real passion for reaching my friends. My walk with Christ became much stronger.

I believe if it were not for the encouragement and prayer support of Mr. Cavill, I would not be where I am today. Mr. Cavill was a man of prayer, and through the eyes of faith he was able to see my potential and to perceive the future plans God had for me. I am sure that Mr. Cavill was cheering us on as my wife, Jenny, and I left our careers in our early twenties and committed ourselves to full-time missionary service. Only God knows how much Mr. Cavill's prayers sustained and carried me through the shaky years of my youth, and beyond that into my years of ministry.

Many people feel that they are not qualified or capable of being mentors. But I believe everyone can at least be a prayer mentor. You don't need any special qualifications to pray for someone. You don't need to feel you have it "all together" to be a prayer mentor. You simply have to be willing to pray for people other than yourself, and to let them know you are praying for them.

It is very affirming (and sometimes convicting) to know someone is praying for you. When Mr. Cavill told me he was praying for me every day, it gave me a sense of self-worth and value. When Mr. Cavill told me he believed that God had something special in store for me, I started to wonder what this meant, and eventually began to believe that God did indeed have something special for me to do in life. In many ways Mr. Cavill's belief in me was prophetic. It was the way in which God conveyed to me that He had a plan for my life and that it would involve some kind of special service for Him.

In his epistles, Paul often mentions his prayer mentoring role. He says to Timothy, "I thank God, whom I serve, as my forefathers did, with a clear conscience, as night and day I constantly remember you in my prayers."[7] And to the Christians in Philippi he says, "I thank my God every time I remember you. In all my prayers for all of you, I always pray with joy because of your partnership in the gospel from the first day until now, being confident of this, that he who began a good work in you will carry it on to completion until the day of Christ Jesus."[8] And he frequently ended his letters by telling his readers how they could pray for him.

Mentoring is all about affirming, encouraging, and nurturing others to be all God wants them to be. Selecting people to pray for, and then letting them know you are praying for them, is not hard to do; and the potential impact that this can have on a person—particularly a young person—can be life changing. It is a great starting point for an ongoing and deepening mentoring relationship.

Peer Mentoring

When I was starting out in my local church pastoral role, one of my first steps was to gather together the core members of the youth group to talk about the development of the church youth ministry. This small group consisted of around fifteen teenagers who were interested in reaching their friends. As we talked over possible strategies, I soon realized that we would not be able to develop an effective youth ministry unless these young people were driving the youth outreach programs and were intimately involved in the process of reaching their peers. It was clear that these enthusiastic and committed teenagers were not interested in perpetuating the traditional church youth ministry model. They were not looking to me and the church to provide programs that kept them occupied and entertained—they seriously wanted to reach their friends.

If they were going to have a say, then things were going to change. So I challenged them to go away and pray, and come back to me in two weeks and tell me if they were prepared to lead the youth ministry of the church with my support. All of them came back with a wholehearted commitment to lead and serve.

With this group of fifteen teenagers leading the youth ministry, we launched into an amazing period of growth and challenge, not only for the youth group, but for the whole church. Over a period of about eighteen months we saw around seventy young people give their lives to Christ and become integrated into the church youth community. The teenagers leading the ministry came up with some amazing strategies for reaching their friends. In the end, though, I don't believe it was the innovative programs or strategies that made their ministry so effective; it was the commitment of these young leaders to mentoring their friends.

This "peer mentoring" aspect of the ministry happened more by default than by design. These young leaders were so committed to reaching their friends and leading them into a relationship with Christ that as soon as one of their friends became a Christian, they would, in a very natural way, start a process of discipleship. And the process was fundamentally a process of mentoring, of modeling the Christian life and walking with the new Christians as they began their journey of discipleship.

The amazing thing was that even the new Christians started to get engaged in the mentoring process. Some who had been Christians for only a few months would take on the responsibility of mentoring their friends who had just made commitments to Christ. And even though they knew they were ill equipped to provide all the answers to those they were mentoring, they would still engage in the mentoring process, knowing there were others in their community further along on the journey of faith from whom they could seek help when they got stuck. I had a constant stream of mentors coming to me with their "mentees," seeking guidance as they came up against issues and challenges that neither of them could resolve.

The mentoring process adopted by these young people was not very complex. It simply involved being good listeners, spending hours with each other chatting about life and faith, serving each other by just being there whenever anyone had a need, exploring the Bible together to find answers to the daily challenges they encountered in living for Jesus, and seeking the counsel of older Christians they trusted when they couldn't find the answers.

Rob and Gary—Discipleship Through Mentoring

Rob was one of the young leaders in the youth group who was very focused on reaching his friends for Jesus. He had recently moved to a new home and had managed to meet a few of the neighbors. One of the nearby families had a son named Gary[9] who was about the same age as Rob. Over the course of several months, Rob discovered—through some conversations with Gary's parents and Gary himself—that Gary was a very troubled young man who had many needs. Gary's parents were at a loss how to help him. Throughout his teenage years Gary had used drugs of all kinds and had also developed a serious dependency on alcohol. He had consistently stolen money, electronics, and household items from his parents' home to fund his addictions. Gary had been so drunk and drug affected one night that he had crashed his car at high speed into a gas station, causing part of the roof structure of the gas station to collapse, trapping the car underneath.

As Rob got to know Gary, he was convinced that God was directing him to reach out to Gary. And so he started spending time with Gary, serving and ministering to him, and sharing with him about his faith in Jesus. At first Gary was very dismissive and showed no interest, but Rob persisted. He eventually invited Gary to come to an outreach Bible study we held for the youth community every Wednesday evening. To Rob's surprise Gary agreed to come, and he kept coming every Wednesday night. Eventually, after many conversations with Rob about Jesus and Christianity, Gary gave his life to Christ.

Gary struggled enormously in his first year as a Christian. Rob naturally transitioned into a peer mentor for him. He walked with him through many struggles and challenges, including helping Gary move from a dependency on drugs and alcohol to a dependency on Jesus. Gary will testify that if it were not for the peer mentoring relationship he had with Rob, he would not have made it through his early years as a follower of Jesus. Rob nurtured and cared for him, did regular Bible studies with him, listened to him for hours, argued with him about issues of faith and life, challenged him about his behavior and values, and protected him and advocated for him when he messed up.

Gary went on to be a leader in the church youth community. He became a lead tenant in the youth accommodation home run by the church, helped numerous other young people find Jesus, and was a very effective peer mentor to many of the new believers. Both his troubled past and his changed life became resources from which he ministered to others. Gary eventually became a pastor and serves today in a pastoral role in a church in Melbourne.

Encouragement and Accountability Through Peer Mentoring
Fostering an environment that encourages peer mentoring is a vital element in effectively reaching young people and developing long-term authentic disciples of Jesus. It not only provides the nurture and support necessary for growing new Christians, but it also enables relationships of mutual accountability to develop. This accountability provides the catalyst for growth and maturity for both people involved in the mentoring relationship. And peer mentoring does not necessarily have to be conducted on a one-on-one basis; it can be just as effective in growing disciples of Christ in a small-group model involving three or four peers.

Anyone at any stage of life will benefit from a peer mentoring relationship. I have found throughout my Christian journey that my peer mentoring relationships have consistently been a key element in my growth and development as a disciple. You and I need accountability not only to continue to grow as Christians but also to stay true to our calling to be salt and light in the world. As you and another believer develop a peer mentoring relationship, you create an environment of trust and mutual accountability, which allows you the freedom to honestly explore the challenges of faith and service to Jesus.

Peer mentoring is one of the best ways I know to foster mutual encouragement, and mutual encouragement is a very strong theme of the New Testament. Here are some examples: "Therefore encourage one another and build each other up, just as in fact you are doing";[10] "But encourage one another daily";[11]

"Let us not give up meeting together, as some are in the habit of doing, but let us encourage one another."[12] Offering encouragement to others ought to be habitual among Christians.

Peer mentoring is similar to prayer mentoring in how easy it is for someone to enter into a peer mentoring relationship. It simply involves finding someone who is at the same stage of life as you are and who has a desire to grow as a Christian. Then you both come to some understanding—or even better, to some kind of formalized agreement—that requires meeting regularly, praying for each other, and keeping each other accountable.

One of the best ways to encourage young people to be involved in peer mentoring relationships is for the Christian community to model peer mentoring to them. Unfortunately, current research shows that less than one out of every six churched believers has a relationship with another believer through which spiritual accountability is provided.[13] Contributing to the growth and spiritual development of young believers requires that we provide models for them to follow. We must demonstrate the practices and lifestyle that they can emulate to continue to grow and mature as disciples of Jesus.

Model Mentoring

In Hebrews 11 the writer presents a list of "heroes of faith," people who gave their all for God. These believers were prepared to live out their faith and remain true to their calling, no matter what the cost. He uses this list of people as "models," encouraging the believers to aspire to be like these faithful and sacrificial servants of God. He states, "Therefore, since we are surrounded by such a great cloud of witnesses, let us throw off everything that hinders and the sin that so easily entangles, and let us run with perseverance the race marked out for us."[14] This kind of "model mentoring" is an essential and strategic element in the development of authentic, faithful, sacrificial, and spiritually mature disciples of Christ. Biblical characters certainly met this criteria, but so do many more mature Christians that we might meet along the way in life.

Providing a Compelling Model to Follow
Jenny and I would not be where we are today in our spiritual walk and ministry life if it were not for the encouragement and nurture of several model mentors. One of our model mentors who played a very strategic role in our spiritual development and commitment to Christian mission was a man named Gordon Blowers.

Gordon was a very successful businessman who, in his early fifties, realized he had spent most of his life building his own kingdom, rather than investing his time, treasure, and talents in God's kingdom. So he gave up his business ventures, and with a group of other people in similar stages of life, started a ministry called Mobile Mission Maintenance (MMM). Gordon had spent most of his life in the building, engineering, and automobile industries. He was a very practical and multi-skilled businessman, and God had given him a vision for utilizing these skills and talents in supporting those who served on the mission field.

Gordon believed that those serving on the mission field should be utilizing all their talents, gifts, and time in doing what God had called them to do, rather than getting distracted and frustrated by trying to develop and maintain the resources to support their ministries. So he recruited many tradespeople to join him in serving those who serve. These teams traveled

all over Australia (and later as the ministry developed, all over
the world), providing help with building, renovating, painting, restoring, auto repairs, electrical installations, and plumb-
ing. MMM supplied skilled general property and equipment
maintenance for missions, churches, and ministries.

Gordon was a member of the church I grew up in. I was
in my late teens when he founded MMM with a number of
other equally committed businessmen. I watched with interest
as Gordon withdrew from his business ventures and gave up
everything to serve others. When Gordon heard that Jenny
and I were interested in mission work, he deliberately went out
of his way to encourage us and spend time with us.

Gordon was regularly asked to speak at local churches
about the ministry of MMM, and he started inviting us to
go with him to these churches. Jenny and I would sing and
he would preach. Many times, in many different church environments, we would listen to Gordon share his story and
challenge people to not waste their lives chasing after things
that had no lasting value, but to chase after God and His will
for their lives.

His messages were always challenging and practical. For example, we were once at a service in a church that was located
in a very wealthy area of Melbourne. In the middle of his message, Gordon stopped and said, "You know, if Jesus came back
tonight and caught us all up in the air to be with Him, I think
He would hover over the church parking lot for a while so that
you could all look back at those expensive cars you are leaving
behind."

Gordon continued to encourage us in our exploration of
mission opportunities. He invited us on an MMM work party

to enable us to get a taste of mission. He introduced us to others who served with him in MMM or in other mission contexts, and they shared their stories with us. When we finally decided to give up our careers and to venture out onto the mission field, he became our advocate and mentor. He helped us through many tough times in our journey into full-time missionary service.

In our first few years of mission, serving in an Aboriginal community on the edge of the desert in Western Australia, Gordon visited us on several occasions, usually bringing MMM work parties with him to help with maintenance and building projects. During each visit, he would spend hours with us, checking on how we were doing and advising and encouraging us in our ministry.

Overall, Gordon provided a powerful and compelling model for us to follow. He didn't just talk about serving God, he lived out his belief and commitment before us. He demonstrated to us what it means to give everything up for Jesus and to invest all of our time, treasure, and talents in God's kingdom. He encouraged us to serve by modeling service to others; he encouraged us to live by faith by living by faith himself; he encouraged us to give generously by giving sacrificially of all he possessed; and he encouraged us to adopt the values of the kingdom of God by applying those values in every area of his life.

Providing an Example to Follow

The apostle Paul practiced model mentoring. To the Corinthians he said, "Follow my example, as I follow the example of Christ."[15] To the believers at Philippi he said, "Join with others in following my example, brothers, and take note of those who live according to the pattern we gave you."[16] And to the Thessalonians he said, "For you yourselves know how you ought to follow our example."[17]

How many of us could say to young believers, "Follow my example, as I follow the example of Christ"? Would we feel confident enough in the authenticity and faithfulness of our own walk with Jesus to be able to offer ourselves as a model for them to follow? I expect that many Christians would answer no to this question. But this is exactly what God requires of us. He wants us to live in such a way that we provide a model to others of how a Christian should live.

Paul and Timothy are the classic biblical example of a model mentoring relationship. But it is interesting to note that in his mentoring relationship with Timothy, Paul didn't focus only on Timothy following his example; he challenged Timothy to take on a mentoring role as well. In his first letter to Timothy Paul says, "Don't let anyone look down on you because you are young, but set an example for the believers in speech, in life, in love, in faith and in purity."[18]

Paul urged not only Timothy but others to take on model mentoring roles. He said to Titus, "In everything set them an example by doing what is good. In your teaching show integrity, seriousness and soundness of speech that cannot be condemned."[19]

We Are All Models for Someone

Young people are looking for heroes, for people they can use as "models" for defining their values and life priorities. Unfortunately, young people consistently look in all the wrong places for these heroes, often modeling their lives on flawed, morally bankrupt sports and entertainment industry stars. But the landscape is changing, and we are now confronted with a rising tide of Christian young people across the world who are no longer looking to the sports and movie stars for values and direction in life. They are looking for models of authentic Christianity. We need to step up to the mark and be the authentic believers these young people need in order to nurture and disciple them.

You may be thinking as you read this that you are just not ready or equipped to be a model mentor, that you haven't got your life together enough to have others follow your example. However, whether we like it or not, at some stage in our lives most of us are going to end up being a model for young people.

Parents, whether they like it not, take on the roles of model mentors. Children model their lives on those of their parents. In their teenage years children very often rebel against their parents' authority and influence, but as they move out of their teenage years into young adulthood, many of the values and life practices they adopt reflect what their parents modeled to them. So for the sake of your children alone, you need to start thinking about what kind of model you are providing—or are going to provide—for young people, and especially for your own children.

As a parent, the model of faith, character, and service you provide for your children has implications that extend well beyond your immediate family, affecting your grandchildren and great-grandchildren. God points out a number of times in the Old Testament the consequences when parents do not provide adequate models for their children. He warns that the sins of fathers will influence and affect the children as far forward as the third and fourth generation.[20]

So the question we all need to answer is not whether we are going to be a model mentor, but what kind of model mentor are we going to be.

Reflecting the Character of Jesus

Jesus is the ultimate model mentor. When He walked on this earth with His disciples, He provided them—and us—with the perfect model to follow. If we truly want to know how we should live, we need to look to Jesus. But Jesus' plan for the discipleship of His people involves us. As His followers, He commissions us to be His representatives in the world. He wants us to live Christlike lives that reflect His character, so that others will come to know Him by seeing Him reflected in us.

Many years ago I heard a story about a missionary doctor serving in a hospital in India. One day one of his patients asked him why he had given up his lucrative and comfortable life in Australia to come and live in such a poor area of the world, to care for people no one else cared about. This doctor saw this as a great opportunity to share Jesus and the message of salvation with this man. After spending several hours explaining who Jesus was and the salvation he offered the world, the man responded, "I don't know this Jesus you are talking about, but if He is anything like you, I want to get to know Him."

To be an effective model mentor we need to be like Jesus. We need to live such authentic lives of faith and service that others will see Jesus in us and be motivated to be more like Jesus themselves.

The dilemma we face is that we are going to need a whole army of model mentors to nurture and care for the wave of young people God is raising up to take this world by storm. Unfortunately, this mentor army is very short on soldiers at present, but God is doing something about this shortage that I believe very few are aware of, and it involves a revolution of global proportions.

Revolutionary Mentors

George Barna has been described as the most quoted person in the Christian church today. For years Barna has been conducting research of the demographical and sociological trends in the Christian church, particularly in America and Western societies. He is one of the most knowledgeable and informed commentators on current trends in the church, and arguably the most accurate predictor of where the church is heading.

In 2005 Barna released a book titled *Revolution*, which provides a detailed analysis of the intersection of social and cultural change and spiritual transformation. In this book, Barna describes a single trend that is redefining faith and the church—an explosion of spiritual energy and activity that he calls the "Revolution." He depicts this new trend as a reengineering of faith, likely to be the most significant transition in the religious landscape that we will ever experience.

Over a period of several years leading up to the writing of this book, Barna devoted much of his energy and research acumen to understanding and accurately measuring this set of radical changes that are reshaping the church. His conclusion is that we are living in a "Revolutionary Age," and at the forefront of the Revolution is a subculture that consists of people who Barna identifies as the "Revolutionaries."

He describes these Revolutionaries as people who are "devout followers of Jesus Christ who are serious about their faith, who are constantly worshiping and interacting with God," people who have a "complete dedication to being thoroughly

Christian by viewing every moment of life through a spiritual lens and making every decision in light of biblical principles. These are individuals who are determined to glorify God every day through every thought, word, and deed in their lives."[21] He goes on to say that what makes these Revolutionaries so unique and world-changing is that they are

> . . . confidently returning to a first-century lifestyle based on faith, goodness, love, generosity, kindness, simplicity, and other values deemed "quaint" by today's frenetic and morally un-tethered standards. This is not the defeatist retreat of an underachieving, low-capacity mass of people. It is the intelligent and intentional embrace of a way of life that is the only viable antidote to the untenable moral standards, dysfunctional relationships, material excess, abusive power, and unfortunate misapplication of talent and knowledge that passes for life in America these days.[22]

Barna sees these Revolutionaries as sojourners who are

> . . . seeking a faith experience that is more robust and awe-inspiring, a spiritual journey that prioritizes transformation at every turn, something worthy of the Creator whom their faith reflects. They are seeking the spark provided by a commitment to a true revolution in thinking, behavior, and experience, where settling for what is merely good and average is defeat. Revolutionaries zealously pursue an intimate relationship with God, which Jesus Christ promised we could have through him. They recognize that there is a huge price to pay in this lifetime—but they are mindful of the eternal pay-off as well.[23]

One of the most startling things that Barna's research has uncovered about what he calls the "Revolutionary sub-nation" is that it already contains well over twenty million people in

America.[24] These are people who are sold out to Jesus, who are living by the principles of the Bible, and who are modeling the practices of the first-century church. Such a large number of Revolutionaries will not remain hidden for long, and their influence will be felt at every level of society. Barna believes that the "Revolution of Faith" that is being led by these Revolutionaries will affect every social institution and every person in America. He asserts that "this is not simply a movement; it is a full scale reengineering of the role of faith in personal lives, the religious community, and the society at large."

Barna's description of the Revolutionaries of America accurately aligns with the characteristics of the emerging generation that God is raising up across the world, the young people who I believe will be at the forefront of the next wave of mission. For example, the young revolutionaries who are engineering and driving the massive societal change in Rwanda exhibit all the attributes of the Revolutionaries of America.

What I find enormously encouraging about Barna's book is that through his research and predictive analysis, he has uncovered what God is doing in the church and in society to prepare the ground for the next wave of mission. The emergence of these Revolutionaries provides a pool of model mentors to disciple and guide the young agents of the kingdom that God is releasing into the world. More than this, through the revolution of the church, God is preparing a fertile and vibrant environment to nurture and empower the enormous harvest of new believers that will be fed into the church as they are impacted by this missional tidal wave.

I believe that if Barna extended his research beyond the borders of the U.S., it would confirm what I have perceived from my encounters with the church in the many nations I have visited across the globe: that these so-called Revolution-aries are springing up worldwide, in every cultural, ethnic, and geographical context.

Barna encourages all Christians to consider becoming revo-lutionaries and to join the Revolution. But becoming a revolu-tionary is not easy; it requires a total realignment of "personal identity." As Barna explains,

> The main reason why most local churches have little influence on the world is that their congregants do not experience this transformation in identity.... Churchgoers are more likely to see themselves as Americans, consumers, professionals, parents, and unique individuals than zealous disciples of Jesus Christ. Until that self-image is reoriented, churches will not have the capacity to change their world.... After all, being a revolutionary is a dan-gerous and demanding undertaking; it is not for the minimally committed.[25]

I believe that adopting this revolutionary life-orientation and new identity in Christ—as so well described by Barna—is essential to being an effective model mentor. My encourage-ment to all who are reading this book is to take up the chal-lenge to be a revolutionary disciple of Jesus—for the sake of your own spiritual well-being, for the sake of the kingdom, and for the sake of the young people of this world.

NOTES

1. Matthew 4:19
2. Galatians 5:22-23
3. Matthew 23:2-3
4. Matthew 23:15
5. Matthew 23:27-28
6. Matthew 18:6
7. 2 Timothy 1:3
8. Philippians 1:3-6
9. Real name withheld for privacy.
10. 1 Thessalonians 5:11
11. Hebrews 3:13
12. Hebrews 10:25
13. George Barna, *Revolution* (Wheaton, IL: Tyndale House, 2005), p. 34.
14. Hebrews 12:1
15. 1 Corinthians 11:1
16. Philippians 3:17
17. 2 Thessalonians 3:7
18. 1 Timothy 4:12
19. Titus 2:7
20. Exodus 20:5; 34:7; Numbers 14:18
21. Barna, p. 8.
22. Barna, p. 12.
23. Barna, pp. 14-15.
24. Barna, p. 13.
25. Barna, pp. 87-88.

CHAPTER EIGHT

PRAYING FOR (AND WITH) THE NEXT WAVE

Rodrigo grew up on the streets of Rio de Janeiro, Brazil. He didn't have much of a family life and at a very early age had to learn to fend for himself, quickly developing the skills necessary to survive on the streets of one of the most populous and crime-ridden cities of the world.

Belonging to the right street gang was one of the keys to survival on the streets, and Rodrigo soon discovered which gang he needed to align himself with to attain the greatest level of status and protection. After joining the local neighborhood branch of one of the largest and most violent gangs in Rio, Rodrigo's natural leadership skills quickly carried him through the hierarchy of leadership. By the time he reached his midteens he was one of the key leaders in the street gang.

Soccer (football) is the national sport of Brazil. The Brazilian people are incredibly passionate about their local teams and every game is a sell-out affair. The street gangs regularly attended soccer games *en masse*, aligning themselves with particular teams. Rodrigo's gang was well represented at every local soccer game. But the gang had more in mind than just cheering their team on at each game they attended. They used these games as the gathering point for gang warfare, and after each game, street battles between rival gangs would erupt outside the stadium.

Rodrigo was responsible for smuggling weapons into the game venue. He hid guns and knives inside drums that the gang members carried into the stadium to beat in support of their team. During the game, the weapons were passed out to the gang members. Immediately following the game Rodrigo led his gang out of the stadium, and—hyped-up on adrenalin, alcohol, and drugs—they entered into enormous battles with other gangs. Many young people were maimed and killed in these battles, but Rodrigo was a survivor and managed to get through every battle virtually unscathed.

One day some women sought out Rodrigo on the streets and introduced themselves as "Prayer Mothers" from Youth for Christ. They told Rodrigo that they were going to specifically pray for him. Rodrigo was not impressed, and told the women that he didn't care whether they prayed for him or not.

It was not long after this encounter with the Prayer Mothers that Rodrigo got into a major street battle with a powerful rival gang. His gang was seriously outnumbered and very soon they were overcome by sheer numbers. As the leader of his gang, Rodrigo was a prime target, and after becoming isolated from the remaining gang members he was severely beaten and stabbed and left for dead. When his fellow gang members found him, he was barely alive. They took him to the local hospital and left him in the emergency area, hoping the hospital would care for him.

The hospital staff did all they could to help him, but he was

so severely injured that it was doubtful whether he would survive. The YFC Prayer Mothers heard what had happened, and
they came to the hospital and started a prayer vigil around
Rodrigo's bed. God miraculously answered their prayers, and
Rodrigo made it through the crisis. As he regained consciousness the first thing he saw was five women kneeling around his
bed praying for him.

I was attending a YFC international conference in Brazil
when I first heard Rodrigo's story. He had been asked to share
his story at a business session attended by all the national
leaders at the conference. He was speaking in Portuguese with
someone translating into English. As he got to the point in
his story where he regained consciousness in his hospital bed,
he stopped speaking in Portuguese, and in faltering English
explained that when he looked into the eyes of these Prayer
Mothers around his bed, he saw the love of Jesus and it melted his heart. Rodrigo then started pointing at various people
in the room whom he had met at the conference, saying, "I see
the same love in the eyes of Rob, and Paul, and Linda." Then
he pointed at me and said, "I see the same love in the eyes of
David." And at that moment I also saw the love of Jesus in
Rodrigo's eyes as he looked at me—and it melted my heart.

Rodrigo was prayed into the kingdom by a handful of ordinary women who, through the power of prayer, were able to do
extraordinary things. I can't imagine any youth ministry that
would design a strategy of sending middle-aged women onto
the streets of Rio to reach the leader of a street gang. But when
we allow God to direct ministry, He continues to surprise us
with how He uses the unexpected and the seemingly illogical
to reach into this world and to love people into His kingdom.

YFC Brazil now has about sixty thousand women who serve as Prayer Mothers in the ministry. These women pray daily for the young people of Brazil, focusing on schools and communities. They target specific young people and pray them into the kingdom. When a young person makes a commitment to Christ, one of the women who has been praying for that youth becomes his or her own Prayer Mother. She commits to discipling and mentoring this young person for a lifetime. Rodrigo's Prayer Mother was with him at the conference, encouraging him and supporting him in prayer as he participated in the young leaders' training program and as he shared his story with the YFC leaders.

After giving his life to Jesus, Rodrigo served for a number of years in YFC as a leader of a team in a suburb of Rio, reaching hundreds of other street gang members with the gospel. He is now a youth pastor of a church in Rio. Rodrigo's Prayer Mother continues today in her mentoring role, supporting Rodrigo in prayer and providing encouragement and counsel.

The extraordinary growth of the YFC ministry in Brazil over recent years directly correlates to the development of the Prayer Mothers ministry. As the Prayer Mothers increased in numbers, so the ministry of YFC grew. Prayer is an absolutely essential element of any effective ministry or mission initiative.

Overcoming Any Obstacle Through Prayer
The Prayer Mothers of Brazil can attest over and over again to God's faithfulness to answer prayers and break down barriers that are an impediment to ministry and mission.

In July 2005, YFC held a conference in Colorado Springs, Colorado. This event brought together the national leaders of YFC from over eighty different nations. Organizing an event like this is a big challenge, particularly when it comes to obtaining visas for all of the delegates.

The year before, the international conference had been held in Brazil. It was at that conference that Rodrigo shared his story. It was a memorable time together for the international family of YFC, and we were especially blessed by the ministry of a group of gifted Brazilian young people who led us in worship in five different languages. Their ministry was so significant that we wanted to bring them to Colorado to once again lead us in worship. However, to obtain one U.S. visitor visa for a Brazilian is very difficult; to obtain six visas for six young adult Brazilians is almost impossible.

Letters of invitation were sent to YFC Brazil, all the paperwork was completed with great care, and our six young Brazilian leaders traveled with one of our senior YFC leaders to the U.S. consulate in Brazil.

At the consulate they were all ushered into the interview office of a U.S. consular official. They passed the invitation letter that we had sent across the desk to the official. He took a brief look at the letter and threw it back at them, stating, "Anyone can write a letter!" He proceeded to grill the young people, asking them about their income, whether they were married, and what jobs they had. All of the members of the worship team were either students or in full-time ministry with YFC. As such they had no guaranteed income, very little money in the bank, no assets—such as a house or property—and no acceptable employment. The consular official was extremely rude and dismissive, and the worship team members watched in stunned silence as this official proceeded to crumple up all of the applications on his desk and throw them into a trash can beside his chair.

The team and their leader didn't know what to do. The official didn't tell them to leave his office, so they just sat there in silence for at least five minutes! All of a sudden the consular official, without saying a word, reached into the trash can and pulled out the applications. He proceeded to meticulously straighten them out one-by-one on his desk and stamp each one as approved. He then handed them back to the YFC leader. Without saying anything more, the young people and their leader left the office with their visas approved.

It wasn't until the worship team returned to the YFC office in Belo Horizonte that they discovered some explanation for this bizarre interview. A number of Prayer Mothers had gathered to pray for the young leaders as they visited the U.S. consulate. At the very moment that the consulate official was retrieving the applications from the trash and approving them, the leader of the Prayer Mothers had gone over to one of the women praying, laid her hand on her head, and said, "Whatever you are praying for now, the Lord has just told me he has answered this prayer." This Prayer Mother had just prayed specifically that God would make the consular official who was interviewing the young people give them their visas!

This miraculous answer to prayer was an enormous encouragement to all of our staff and volunteers in Brazil, as well as many others around the world who were also trying to get visas. It was a reminder that God is in charge, that He does answer prayer in miraculous ways, and that nothing can stop Him from achieving His purposes.

Prayer Support

Anyone in ministry leadership knows the value of prayer support. Without the prayers of the ministry partners who stand with us in our ministry, there is no way we could fulfill our calling and achieve all that God requires of us.

There is an account in Exodus 17 of a battle between the Israelites and the Amalekites at a place called Rephidim.[1] As the battle took place, Moses stood on a hill overlooking the valley of Rephidim and held up his staff in both his hands. As long as Moses held up his hands, the Israelites were winning; but as the battle progressed Moses became very tired and lowered his hands. As soon as he lowered his hands the Amalekites started to overcome the Israelites and win the battle. So Aaron and Hur took a large stone and put it on the top of the hill so Moses could sit on it. They then got on both sides of Moses and held up his hands right through the day until the battle was won.

When you pray for people in ministry, particularly those in leadership, you are playing a similar role to that of Aaron and Hur. You are "holding up the arms" of those you are praying for and allowing them to be victorious in the battles that God has sent them to fight. It is a humbling and affirming thing to know that people are praying for you. I know for a fact that whenever I receive any kind of credit for what I do in ministry, it can only be attributed to the people who faithfully stand with me in prayer, and to our God who faithfully answers those prayers.

Paul points out the importance of prayer for his ministry. He asks the Ephesians to "pray in the Spirit on all occasions with all kinds of prayers and requests. With this in mind, be alert and always keep on praying for all the saints. Pray also for me, that whenever I open my mouth, words may be given me so that I will fearlessly make known the mystery of the gospel, for which I am an ambassador in chains. Pray that I may declare it fearlessly, as I should."[2]

You only have to look at the life of Jesus to know how important prayer is for effective ministry. Jesus consistently spent hours in prayer—particularly prior to or following a significant ministry moment or challenge—modeling for us the essential nature of prayer for effective and powerful ministry.

Failures of God's people recorded in the Bible also teach us a lot about the importance of prayer. When the people of Israel failed miserably in their attack on a city called Ai, it was because they did not consult God and ask for His blessing on their endeavors.[3] In the same way, when the disciples failed in ministry, Jesus pointed out that it was due to a lack of prayer.[4]

Partnership in Prayer

God's plan for us is to work in unity and partnership with other believers, and it is only as we combine our talents and gifts in a concerted effort that we will be able to represent our God on this earth and operate effectively as a community of believers. In 1 Corinthians Paul uses the example of the human body to explain the synergistic importance of believers' work in unison, combining their multifaceted gifts and talents.

> Now the body is not made up of one part but of many. If the foot should say, "Because I am not a hand, I do not belong to the body," it would not for that reason cease to be part of the body. And if the ear should say, "Because I am not an eye, I do not belong to the body," it would not for that reason cease to be part of the body. If the whole body were an eye, where would the sense of hearing be? If the whole body were an ear, where would the sense of smell be? But in fact God has arranged the parts in the body, every one of them, just as he wanted them to be. If they were all one part,

where would the body be? As it is, there are many parts, but one body. The eye cannot say to the hand, "I don't need you!" And the head cannot say to the feet, "I don't need you!"[5]

Just as it would be ridiculous for an ear or an eye to think that it could function without the rest of the body, so it is ridiculous to think that anyone can serve in a ministry role isolated from the rest of the body of Christ. And this is particularly the case when it comes to prayer. Anyone in ministry who does not have the prayer backing of other members of God's family will be as ineffective as an ear or an eye without the rest of the body.

The emerging generation of missional leaders will not be able to function without substantial prayer support and partnership. We must get behind them in prayer. The rest of the church cannot just simply sit back as observers and spectators, watching this wave of mission sweep across the globe. We have a vital and strategic role to play as prayer warriors in the battle for the lives of millions. Paul urges us to support others through prayer, to "pray in the Spirit on all occasions with all kinds of prayers and requests. With this in mind, be alert and always keep on praying for all the saints."[6]

Let us rally around and hold up the arms of these young leaders. If we don't, as they grow weary and powerless due to lack of prayer support, there is a great danger that the battle will turn against them, just as it did for Moses and the people of Israel.

Prayer Triplets
Our prayer support for this emerging generation of revolutionary young leaders is vital. But it's also vital to help *them* pray. One of the most effective strategies I have seen employed

for motivating and enabling young people to pray is "Prayer Triplets." The Prayer Triplet strategy has been utilized effectively by YFC throughout the world to mobilize tens of thousands of young people to pray. It is such an effective strategy that I am going to take some time to explain how it works.

A Prayer Triplet is made up of a group of three young Christians committed to praying together regularly. It requires one young person to take a lead role. This leader recruits two other young people to join his or her Triplet, and then coordinates the Prayer Triplet gatherings and keeps the team on track.

Young people who are interested in leading a Prayer Triplet are asked to consider four questions:

1. Are you aware of your responsibility to speak often with God about the world in which you live?

2. Are you convinced that prayer takes on special significance when it is undertaken with other Christians?

3. Are you ready to learn how you can help others as well as yourself develop an effective prayer life?

4. Do you know at least two other people who would answer yes to the above questions?

It is surprising how many young people will answer yes to these four questions. Yet many young Christians do not spend a lot of time in prayer. This is not because young people are unwilling to pray, or that they don't care about their friends enough to pray for them, or even that they are not interested in praying for the world. The reason why many young people are not engaged in prayer is because no one is challenging them to pray or providing models for them to help them to be consistent and organized in their prayer life.

The Prayer Triplet strategy prescribes a prayer team of three members because a smaller group better provides a safe environment for sharing at a deep level. Young people are not so nervous about saying the wrong thing in a group of two or three friends, all learning to trust God and each other together. Jesus made some specific promises to pairs and trios who gather together to pray. He promised, "If two of you on earth agree about anything you ask for, it will be done for you by my Father in heaven. For where two or three come together in my name, there am I with them."[7] Another value of limiting the group to three members is that it is small enough to be a very efficient team, but still big enough to be an effective team. As the author of Ecclesiastes wrote, "Though one may be overpowered, two can defend themselves. A cord of three strands is not quickly broken."[8]

The members of each Prayer Triplet are asked to make a specific agreement with each other, and they hold each other accountable for the promises made. They agree to meet for prayer, and their times together are mostly devoted to actually praying rather than to discussing prayer points (which can be a tendency when people gather together to pray). I have often been at prayer meetings where we spend twenty-five minutes discussing prayer items and then only five minutes praying. The main purpose of a Prayer Triplet is to pray.

Prayer Triplets generally meet for thirty minutes once a week. The times together are structured in such a way that the team spends at least twenty minutes in prayer. Regular and frequent meetings help the team members grow and mature in their prayer life. The quantity and quality of the team's prayer time together builds mutual trust and a collective sensitivity of God's purpose and will for their lives.

The prayers of a Prayer Triplet focus on three areas: the spiritual growth of each member of the group and their respective churches, the salvation of group members' friends, and the worldwide work of God.

The first goal of a Prayer Triplet is that each member of the group will come to know Jesus better and will grow to be more like Him. Members will pray for the needs of each other and the challenges that they are experiencing in their lives. The group also prays for the church that each member attends, specifically praying that their church community will grow in spiritual maturity, unity, and authenticity.

The second goal of a Prayer Triplet is to pray for three non-Christian friends of each team member. This means that the team will be praying—by name—for the salvation of nine people. These prayers focus on asking God to reveal what His plan is for each of these friends, and how specifically He wants the members of the group to be involved in sharing His love and salvation with these nine young people. Praying in this way brings a new sensitivity to the work of God in both the lives of the members of the Prayer Triplet and their non-Christian friends.

Finally, the Prayer Triplet members pray for the worldwide work of God. They are encouraged as a team to select three nations of the world to pray for, and they then direct their prayer support to specific ministries and people in these nations.

I have seen these Prayer Triplets transform the lives of the young people involved. When young people get together to pray, their simple trust in Jesus and faith in His promises provides a fertile environment for answered prayer. Miracles of grace and salvation are the products of these Prayer Triplets.

Very often all of the nine friends being prayed for come to faith in Jesus.

Although the Prayer Triplets strategy was designed to serve young people, I believe it has far broader application. I think there would be enormous benefit in employing the same strategy for adult members of a church community. Imagine what would happen if all the adults of a church committed to a Prayer Triplet and prayed weekly for their own spiritual growth (and that of their church), for three of their non-Christian friends to come to Christ, and for God to intervene in three nations of the world. The church community would be transformed. The mutual accountability and solidarity provided by a group of three peers, the focus on personal spiritual growth and integrity, the encouragement to select three friends who need Christ and to weekly bring these friends before God, the commitment to pray for the local church, and the encouragement to look beyond the local context of the group members to the needs of others in the world—how could this not bring about enormous individual and corporate blessing in a church?

To be disciple-makers, we need to be disciples. To lead young people into a God-honoring lifestyle, we need to model that lifestyle. To guide young people into an effective prayer life, we need to go before them practicing what we preach. Prayer is not an option for us; it is demanded of us as followers of Jesus. Spending thirty minutes with two other believers each week, praising God for who He is, and praying for the salvation of others is a good start at modeling what the Bible requires of all believers.

NOTES

1. Exodus 17:8-13
2. Ephesians 6:18-20
3. Joshua 7
4. Mark 9:28-29
5. 1 Corinthians 11:14-21
6. Ephesians 6:18
7. Matthew 18:19-20
8. Ecclesiastes 4:12

CHAPTER NINE

MAKING APPRENTICES
AMONG THE NEXT WAVE

There is a story told of a man who was traveling through the western states of the U.S. As he came to the outskirts of a small town he noticed something unusual. A number of the buildings had targets painted on them, and in the very center of each target was an arrow. The farther he traveled into the town, the more targets he saw—some on buildings, some on light poles and tree trunks—all with an arrow right in the middle of the bull's-eye. He thought, *How can this be? How could someone be so accurate with a bow and arrow?*

He asked around the town to find out who was responsible for such accurate archery, and he continued to get the same answer: "Oh, that's the work of Old Joe. He shoots those arrows." Fascinated, the traveler sought out this man, eager to meet him and hear his story. He started to speculate: "Maybe Old Joe used to be a star archer; possibly he used to perform in a Wild West show, or maybe he was an Olympian and won an Olympic gold medal in archery."

Finally the traveler found someone who knew where Old Joe could be found. They directed him to the local bar, saying

that Old Joe always hung out there in the afternoon and evening. It didn't take long for the traveler to locate the bar. After
asking around, he was sent to a dark corner of the room, where
a solitary figure sat at a small table with a bunch of empty
glasses in front of him. A long bow and a quiver full of arrows
were leaning against the wall next to the table.

As the traveler neared the table, he was confronted with a
disheveled old man who was obviously very drunk. He tried to
strike up a conversation with him, but Old Joe was so drunk it
was difficult to get him to even string two words together, let
alone a whole sentence.

Frustrated, the traveler left the old drunken archer and went
up to the counter to talk to the bartender. He explained that
since seeing the targets and arrows, he had been looking for
Old Joe. And then he asked the bartender the obvious question: "How can such a drunken old man shoot so accurately?"
With a knowing look the barman explained, "Old Joe is a
hopeless archer; he walks around town shooting arrows aimlessly. Sometimes they hit a building, or a post, or a tree—but
we like the old fellow so much that we go around after him and
paint targets wherever the arrows strike!"

Jesus told us to go into the world and make disciples; but
what kind of disciples are we making? As I and other YFC
leadership staff have interacted with churches all over the world,
we have found very few that have a discipleship "target" for
the youth in their church. Many have very extensive activity-
based programs that measure their success on criteria such as
attendance numbers, outreach activities, music and worship
style, entertainment value, and cultural relevance.

There is nothing wrong with providing youth programs

that are culturally relevant and attractive to youth, but without all the activities and programs being grounded and referenced in a model of discipleship and Christian character formation, the youth ministry will be largely aimless. Developing programs solely around the cultural and social interests and needs of youth is just like the people of Old Joe's town painting targets around the arrows he aimlessly shot. The targets were defined by wherever Old Joe shot his arrows. If the youth culture and proclivities of youth are the sole determiners used to set the targets of a church or parachurch youth ministry, then all the youth program will tend to do is reinforce the cultural norms of the young people involved in the program. This approach will result in very little real change and character development.

Because our mandate from Jesus is to make disciples, we need to work out what the end product looks like. We need to set a target that defines the characteristics of a mature and authentic disciple of Jesus, and then we need to aim our youth programs at that target. A "disciple-making" target should not be limited to defining the desired outcome of a youth program of a church; it should be the focal point of the whole church community.

Profile of a Disciple
In my leadership role with Youth for Christ, I am constantly grappling with the challenges of developing and implementing relevant youth outreach programs that will enable us to effectively take the gospel to unreached young people worldwide. However, over the past few years God has taken YFC through a process of soul-searching and spiritual renewal, culminating in a realignment of the primary focus of our ministry.

For over sixty years YFC has been very effective in reaching young people and challenging them to make a commitment to Christ; but God has clearly directed YFC to move from making "converts" to making "disciples"; to not only reach "unreached" young people, but to continue to be engaged in the process of nurturing and discipling these young people.

One of the biggest challenges we faced after going through this God-directed renovating and renewal process, was to come up with a global ministry strategy that would enable us to follow God's mandate to "make disciples." We spent several years developing a comprehensive "Global Ministry Plan" that reflected our new values and emphasis on discipleship. But as we started to implement the plan to make disciples of young people all over the world, we realized that there was a significant strategic flaw. Although we knew we needed to make disciples, we had not actually defined what a disciple looked like. We did not have a specific target to aim at. So after much prayer and thought we developed a "Profile of a Disciple."[1] Through an exhaustive study and application of God's Word, we defined our "end product," listing the attributes of an authentic, world-changing disciple of Christ.

This "profile" impacted every level of the implementation process of our Global Ministry Plan. Armed with the profile we were able to ask the question, "What do we need to put in place to grow this sort of disciple?" The profile was used as a point of reference for all of our planning, enabling us to keep keenly focused on the "why" behind the "what" of our youth programs. Keeping the final target clearly before us, we were able to be far more rigorous in our planning process by constantly assessing our ideas and strategies with the question,

"How is this going to enable us to be more effective in growing young people into this sort of disciple?"

Having the Right Map

Stephen Covey, in his book *The Seven Habits of Highly Effective People*, uses the example of a misprinted map when explaining the importance of having the right value set to navigate life. He sets up a situation in which someone is trying to find a certain place in downtown Chicago. They have a correct address but are using a map for Detroit to find it:

> Can you imagine the frustration, the ineffectiveness of trying to reach your destination?
>
> You might work on your behavior—you could try harder, be more diligent, double your speed. But your efforts would only succeed in getting you to the wrong place faster.
>
> You might work on your attitude—you could think more positively. You still wouldn't get to the right place, but perhaps you wouldn't care. Your attitude would be so positive, you'd be happy wherever you were.
>
> The point is, you'd still be lost. The fundamental problem has nothing to do with your behavior or your attitude. It has everything to do with having a wrong map.
>
> If you have the right map of Chicago, then diligence becomes important, and when you encounter frustrating obstacles along the way, then attitude can make a real difference. But the first and most important requirement is the accuracy of the map.[2]

Making disciples requires that we have the right map, that we know where we are going, and that we know how to get there.

In Covey's example he assumes that we at least know where we want to go. However, it would appear from even a cursory examination of ministry leadership in the church—particularly youth ministry—the "destination" is often unknown or poorly defined.

Let's assume that our desire is to make disciples. Then obviously our "destination" is spiritual maturity for those whom God has given into our care. Clearly defining what a spiritually mature authentic disciple of Jesus looks like is the first step to making disciples. But once our discipleship target is well defined, the next and very important step is mapping out how to get to this destination.

If we use a map for youth ministry based on an entertainment and attendance matrix, we might very well end up with large numbers of young people all having a great time at our youth programs. However, because we are following the wrong map, the young people in these programs are not going to get any closer to the destination of authentic Christianity and spiritual maturity. In fact, they are probably going to end up more lost.

But let's say we use a map that consists of the values and principles that will lead people closer to an authentic walk with Christ—a map that has the road of biblical literacy, the street of prayer, the avenue of forgiveness, the central parkway of *agape* love, the circle of grace, the pathway of relational evangelism, and the driveway of faith. Using this map, our journey with these young people is going to be a whole lot more fulfilling, because it is going to take us, along with these young people, progressively closer to Jesus and a deeply authentic relationship with Him.

Having culturally relevant and attractive programs for young people is important, and we need to package our discipleship process in creative and innovative programs that keep young people engaged. But if we are truly serious about Jesus' call to make disciples, then everything we do should be designed to take the people in our care further along the pathway to spiritual authenticity and maturity.

Apprentices of Christ
Dallas Willard is one of the most significant and prominent leaders of the "Spiritual Formation Movement" that is rapidly gaining momentum across the world. Willard identifies well the challenges facing church leadership in moving away from programmatic and statistics-oriented measurement to a spiritual-formation orientation. He states, "Pastors need to redefine success. The popular model of success involves the ABCs—attendance, buildings, and cash. Instead of counting Christians, we need to weigh them. We weigh them by focusing on the most important kind of growth—love, joy, peace, long-suffering, gentleness, goodness, kindness, and so on—fruit in keeping with the gospel and the kingdom."[3]

Measuring the success of a Christian ministry or church by the character of the people the ministry serves is a fairly uncommon practice. But if we are going to be successful in making disciples of Christ, we need to measure our success by the end product, by how well those we minister to measure up to the values of God's kingdom.

Willard now seldom uses the term *disciple* to describe a follower of Jesus, because he believes the word has lost a lot of its original meaning through misuse and overuse. He prefers to describe followers of Jesus as *apprentices*. He explains, "I like the word *apprentice* because it means I'm with Jesus learning to do what He did. When you look at the first disciples, that's what they were doing. They watched Jesus and listened to Him, and then He said, 'Now you do it.'"[4]

Webster's Dictionary defines an apprentice as "one bound by indenture to serve another for a prescribed period with a view to learning an art or trade; one who is learning by practical experience under skilled workers a trade, art, or calling; an inexperienced person; a novice." In the light of this definition, I agree with Willard: apprentice is a good term to use to describe what being a disciple is all about.

Novices Versus "the Arrived"

The first thing we need to realize in our discipleship journey is that we are novices. The main flaw of the Pharisees—that Jesus consistently condemned—was their self-righteousness. They thought they had "arrived," that they had it all together, and that they were a cut above the "ordinary" people. This is why Jesus said to them, "It is not the healthy who need a doctor, but the sick. I have not come to call the righteous, but sinners."[5] The Pharisees thought they were spiritually healthy and therefore didn't need what Jesus had to offer. They believed when it came to godliness and authentic faith, they had arrived. And although Jesus regularly pointed out their spiritual bankruptcy, the Pharisees continued to fail to recognize their "novice" spiritual status; thus Jesus was unable to help them in their spiritual malaise.

If we are going to grow at all in our spiritual life, we need to first recognize our inexperienced, novice status. When you believe you have "arrived," you have nowhere else to go and no motivation or reason to grow beyond where you are.

There are two reasons why we may believe that we have arrived. The first is that we are in a state of self-righteousness, which was the Pharisees' problem. We think we have got it all together, and that we are so far ahead of the rest of the crowd we don't need to change anything. This is usually a problem associated with those in leadership, and it comes with a good dose of self-deception to complement the self-righteousness. There is not the remotest possibility that people in this state will ever consider themselves as novices.

The second reason we may feel that we have arrived is because we think we have come far enough along on our journey of discipleship that we don't need to travel any further. We have done enough to get into heaven, and we do enough to maintain our Christian status by going to church and giving a donation each week. We have arrived at a point in our lives where we are comfortable and we don't want to travel any further. This is the most common form of the "arrival syndrome." If we are in this state of arrival, we also will not consider ourselves a novice. In fact, most people in this state have been Christians for many years, and they almost universally equate their spiritual maturity to the length of time they have been Christians.

Dallas Willard, whom I would consider a very mature Christian, still presents himself as an apprentice with a long way to go. He says, "As an apprentice of Christ, I may be saved by grace, but I still have years of habitual anger, materialism, lust, and many other things to be dealt with. They're not just going to go away. Like someone who has a bad golf swing and always slices off to the right, I'm going to have to practice hitting the ball in a different way to make it go straight. The slice is in my body; it's how I have been formed. The (spiritual) disciplines help transform my habitual actions. The disciplines are not a substitute for grace, but receptacles for it."[6]

Being aware we are novices, recognizing we need to grow and have much to learn, is the starting point of an apprenticeship with Christ. But we also need to recognize that there will always be more growing ahead, that we are pilgrims on a lifetime of growth in Christian character. In fact, if we are a "growing" Christian, we will never feel comfortable and content. It is extremely uncomfortable to be constantly changing and growing, and there are many "growing pains" associated with becoming an authentic disciple of Christ.

Remember, part of the dictionary definition of the word *apprentice* is "one bound by indenture to serve another for a prescribed period with a view to learning an art or trade." To be an apprentice it is not enough to know that we are unskilled novices; there also needs to be an associated desire and commitment to learn an art or trade. If an apprentice wishes to serve under a particular master, then he or she needs to "sign up" for that service for a certain period of time. When we sign up with Jesus, the prescribed period of "indenture" is "for all eternity."

So, let's say we recognize that we are novices, and desiring to move on from this novice and unskilled state, we indenture ourselves as apprentices of Jesus, the ultimate Master Craftsman. We do so by committing ourselves to a life of self-sacrifice, self-discipline, and subservience to our Master. Once so indentured, how do we model our lives and the practice of our Christian tradecraft after the Master?

WWJD

The question "What would Jesus do?" was first coined by Congregationalist pastor Charles Sheldon in a book he wrote in

1896. In the late 1980s, several youth pastors at various churches in the state of Michigan, in an attempt to encourage their young people to live more like Jesus, adopted Sheldon's phrase and started using the initials "W.W.J.D." as an inscription on badges and bracelets, which they distributed to their young people. The concept was very quickly picked up by Christian merchandisers across the United States and the WWJD movement took off. By the early 1990s, the WWJD movement had spread across the English-speaking world, with millions wearing wrist bands, necklaces, badges, caps, and bracelets to remind them to act like Jesus in their day-to-day lives.

As we wrestle with the challenges associated with being an indentured apprentice of Jesus, I think we can learn some things from the WWJD movement. The WWJD movement was a worthy attempt to encourage people to develop Christian authenticity and integrity. But as pervasive as this movement was in the church in English-speaking Western nations, it seemed to have little spiritual depth or any lasting influence on the capacity of people to live more like Jesus.

Clearly the WWJD strategy had limitations; but we can always learn from the shortcomings of a strategy, particularly if we understand the nature of the limitations. Asking the WWJD question of ourselves as a guide to living like Jesus assumes that we know how Jesus would respond to the complex life situations that we face daily. I believe that this is more of a challenge than what we may first think.

First, Jesus was profoundly unpredictable. His disciples were often caught off guard by Jesus' behavior, teaching, and responses to people. Simply put—it is hard to know the mind of Jesus. Can we really say with confidence that we know how Jesus would respond to the things we face each day?

Second, to express the depth of love, grace, humility, insight, and righteousness that Jesus expressed is a "big ask" using the formulaic process demanded by the WWJD strategy.

Using formulas is not a good way to apply the values of God's kingdom to your life—just ask the Pharisees. The Pharisees had a whole bunch of formulas and rules that they developed, with the idea that by following these rules they—and the people they led—would be able to live as God wanted them to live. This formulaic approach clearly didn't work for the Pharisees. Jesus says to them, "You brood of vipers, how can you who are evil say anything good? For out of the overflow of the heart the mouth speaks."[7]

The Bible consistently talks about spiritual fruit and the character of Christ coming from a changed heart. For instance, "The good man brings good things out of the good stored up in his heart, and the evil man brings evil things out of the evil stored up in his heart. For out of the overflow of his heart his mouth speaks."[8] The heart is the inner core of a person's being, and unless this is transformed and the fruit and grace of God flow naturally from this inner core, then it will be enormously difficult to respond to life situations with the values and character of Christ.

Many of life's events happen without warning, making it very difficult to "prepare" appropriate godly responses. Our reaction to most things we encounter in life is instinctive rather than planned, particularly the things that we find offensive or hurtful. Unfortunately, our instincts are often based on our own flawed values, needs, and desires, rather than on the pure motives of Jesus.

To live as Jesus would have us live is more an issue of *intimacy* than of formulas. Expressing the character and goodness of Jesus in all we do and say demands a special closeness to Him—a deep level of intimacy. Knowing Jesus must take on a much more pervasive effect than simply an awareness of events from His life. There needs to be more of Jesus and far less of us in our lives. This is what Paul was driving at when he says in Philippians 2:13, "For it is God who works in you to will and to act according to his good purpose." As we spend more and more time with Jesus, He will identify the areas of our lives that we are holding back and He will take over more and more of our lives. The secret to living as Jesus would live is to live in a state of constant awareness of Jesus' presence in your life and mine. Only then will we be able to instinctively respond as Jesus would to every life situation, because it will be Jesus who is responding through us.

In 1913 Kate B. Wilkinson wrote a poem that became a beloved hymn. I think it aptly sums up this concept of allowing Jesus to live through us:

> May the mind of Christ, my Savior,
> Live in me from day to day,
> By His love and power controlling
> All I do and say.

> May the Word of God dwell richly
> In my heart from hour to hour,
> So that all may see I triumph
> Only through His power.

> May the peace of God my Father
> Rule my life in everything,
> That I may be calm to comfort
> Sick and sorrowing.

May the love of Jesus fill me,
As the waters fill the sea;
Him exalting, self abasing—
This is victory.

May I run the race before me,
Strong and brave to face the foe,
Looking only unto Jesus
As I onward go.

May His beauty rest upon me
As I seek the lost to win,
And may they forget the channel,
Seeing only Him.

This level of closeness to Jesus can only be achieved by making our relationship with Jesus an absolute priority. We need to be disciplined in our prayer life, spending exclusive and substantial time with Jesus, talking things over with Him and listening to His voice. We need to make spending time with Jesus more important than doing things for Jesus. And we need to be accountable for the time we spend with Jesus, making deliberate changes and setting up accountability structures that ensure those changes.

Quality Means Quantity

Authentic Christian faith is expressed in our relationships—our relationship with Jesus, our relationship with fellow Christians, our relationship with our spouse and children, and our relationship with others outside of God's family. It is how we conduct these relationships that determines our capacity to represent Jesus and to live as He lived.

I am sure that you have heard the term *quality time*. Spending "quality time" with our spouse or children is often presented as a relational panacea, as the "cure-all" to healthy relationships. But from my experience the *quality* of the time we spend with family members is directly related to the *quantity* of time we spend with them. Availability is a key factor in family relationships, because the amount of time we are prepared to devote to being available in a relationship conveys the priority we place upon that relationship.

Let me explain by using the example of the modern family. People's lives today are replete with activities and commitments. In fact, if you ask people how life is going, they will often answer with one word: "busy." By the time families get to the stage of life when the children are in their teenage years, the parents, particularly fathers, are usually so busy in their career and other activities that they have very little time available for their children.

James Dobson talks about this inane busyness:

> The harried lifestyle that characterizes most Westerners leads not only to the isolation of people from each other in the wider community; it is also the primary reason for the breakdown of the family. Husbands and wives have no time for each other and many of them hardly know their children. They don't get together with relatives, friends or neighbors because they are tyrannized by a never-ending "to do" list. Repeatedly during my research ... I came face-to-face with the same sad phenomenon. Parents were simply too distracted and exhausted to protect and care for their children.[9]

In the context of this time-gobbling lifestyle, parents often grab hold of the notion that spending "quality time" with their children will make up for the little time they are available in the home. So they plan an activity to do with their teenage son or daughter that they believe will provide some "bonding" time with their child.

Let's say a father allocates some time in his busy schedule to go to a movie with his teenage son, thinking this will enable them to have some quality time together. Unfortunately, the most likely response the father will receive to his offer will be a dismissive rejection of the whole idea. The reason given will probably be that his son already has other plans—or will be making plans—to do something with his friends.

The fact that the father has planned some "cool" activity with his son means very little to his child, because the activity is not offered in the context of a meaningful relationship with his father. What the son is looking for is a relationship in which he knows he is a priority and knows that he matters more to his father than work or other commitments. He is looking for a father who will be available when he needs help with problems, or a lift to his friend's house, or a chat about something that happened at school. He wants a father who won't just brush him off saying he is too busy when his son needs him. The quality of the relationship is directly proportional to the quantity of time the father is available and willing to spend with his son.

When our daughter, Belinda, was in her midteens, our parental relationship with her became very tense and distant. Belinda was exploring life as a teenager and we were struggling to make sense of her behavior. One day, she simply refused to get up and go to school. She had been sick on and off for several months, but she seemed well enough that day to be able to get out of bed and go to school.

Jenny was the director of a preschool and, being the only

qualified teacher, was unable to stay home at such short notice. And so it was up to me to deal with the problem if Belinda continued to refuse to go to school. I explained to Belinda that I didn't have time to argue with her because I had some extremely important meetings to attend all week and I was going to be late if she didn't get out of bed and get to school. But when Jenny and I pressured her further to get out of bed, she replied, "It's not that I won't get out of bed, it's that I can't."

At that moment in my relationship with my daughter I had a choice, and it had to do with the priorities I placed on my time and relationships. I could have told Belinda, "Okay, stay in bed, rest up, and see how you feel in the evening." But this illness had been going on for a long time, and it was obvious to me that Belinda really had something seriously wrong with her. I could see the desperation in her eyes.

By the grace of God, I realized that I needed to be there for my daughter more than I needed to be at these "crucial" meetings. So I said to Belinda, "You know how important these meetings are, but you are way more important to me than those meetings. I am not sure what they are going to do without me being there to meet with all these people, but I am going to call my office and tell them that I am not coming in, and they will just have to either cancel or reschedule the meetings."

I didn't return to the office for the rest of the week. Belinda and I spent several days running around from doctor to doctor, testing facility to testing facility, and back to the doctors again. But we finally got to the bottom of the illness, and Belinda was able to get the treatment she needed.

Giving up an important meeting and being available for my daughter when she needed me most was a major turning point in our relationship. From that moment on we spent more and more time together, and the quality of the time we spent together seemed to increase proportionally with the amount of time we were together.

The same principles that apply to our relationships with other human beings apply to our relationship with Jesus. The quality of our relationship with Jesus depends upon the quantity of time we spend with Him. We need to be spending as much time as possible with Jesus, striving to be as close to Him as we can, so that He will be reflected in our lives. Busyness not only prevents us from having healthy relationships with our family and friends, but it also prevents us from having an intimate and life-changing relationship with Jesus. Prioritizing our lives around Jesus is the key to being His true representation to the world.

You can't allocate times and dates in your calendar to accommodate a crisis with your son or daughter, or schedule the times that your children will need your advice because they are facing a major challenge. It simply won't work for you to say to your daughter, "Honey, I have an opening on Thursday evening between dinner and my leadership meeting at the church. Can we schedule for you to have a crisis in your relationship with your friend between 7:00 and 7:30 p.m. on Thursday?" Crises in your family members' lives generally come at the most inconvenient times. If you are going to faithfully serve your family, then your spouse and children need to have a place of priority in your life and take precedence over the other items in your weekly schedule.

In the same way, if you are going to faithfully serve Jesus, spending time with Him must take priority in your life. You can't just allocate a free slot here and there in your schedule for Jesus and expect that will provide the relational connection you need to reach a level of spiritual maturity where people will see only Jesus and not you. Jesus is not going to be able to do much in your life if you tell Him, "Well, this week I have an opening on Saturday at 7:30 a.m. when I can spend ten minutes with You." Our relationship with Jesus should be pervasive; it should invade all areas of our lives, not just a five- or ten-minute slot every so often.

Many years ago my mother used to support a ministry that would send her gifts in response to her sending donations to them. These gifts included things such as pendants, ornaments, plaques, and trinkets with quotes from the person who headed up this ministry printed on them. The day she stopped supporting this ministry was the day she received a fridge magnet that stated, "Make time to fit God into your plans."

Unfortunately, this is how many Christians live, fitting God into their plans rather than fitting into God's plans. In the context of our busyness, this is a recipe for spiritual bankruptcy. This is like saying to God, "Well, I have got my life all planned out, but I want You to know that I have put You into my plans, so how about endorsing what I have worked out for my life?" This is not how our relationship with Jesus is meant to be. When we become Christians, we hand our lives over to Jesus and let Him have control. Our relationship with Jesus is an all-or-nothing relationship. Jesus won't have it any other way!

Walking with Jesus Daily

After running a school program in a local high school, David— a YFC leader in Western Australia—visited a supermarket to purchase some groceries. While David was in the store, a young guy came up to him and identified himself as one of the students that had been in the school program. As they were chatting about the program, this high school student—who was not a Christian—noticed the WWJD wristband that David was wearing, and stated, "I know what WWJD means."

David was intrigued. How could this young guy know what WWJD meant, when he didn't seem to have any church background or know much about what is involved in being a follower of Christ? So David asked him what WWJD stands for. The reply surprised and challenged him: "It means Walk With Jesus Daily!" What this young guy came up with was a far more appropriate meaning for the acronym WWJD. If applied, this slogan would be much more effective in enabling a follower of Jesus to live as Jesus lived, rather than trying to follow a formula of working out what Jesus might or might not do in every situation.

Walking with Jesus daily is the best way to answer the question, "What would Jesus do?" Intimacy with Jesus allows us to be sensitive to His leading and direction in our lives, and it gives Him the freedom to live through us.

Pray Continuously

In 1 Thessalonians 5:17 we are instructed to "pray continually." What does Paul mean by this? Obviously he did more than pray all day. Yet what he conveys in this directive seems to suggest that we should be constantly in prayer.

The *Zondervan NIV Bible Commentary* provides a helpful explanation of this verse: " 'Continually' does not mean nonstop praying. Rather, it implies constantly recurring prayer, growing out of a settled attitude of dependence on God. Whether words are uttered or not, lifting the heart to God while one is occupied with miscellaneous duties is the vital thing. Verbalized prayer will be spontaneous and will punctuate one's daily schedule, as it did Paul's writings."[10]

The *Asbury Bible Commentary* provides further insight: "Prayer is the constant attitude of the believer. To 'pray continually' means that every activity must be carried on with a sense of God's presence."[11] This verse is about intimacy in our relationship with Christ, living in an attitude of prayer that provides a continuous connection with our God and Savior. Spending time with Jesus deepens your relationship with Him and allows this intimacy to develop.

When I was starting out in my ministry with YFC, I was concerned that I was not spending enough time in prayer. I wanted to get closer to Jesus and develop a deeper understanding of His plan for my life. At the same time, I realized I needed to improve my fitness. So I also decided to start walking for an hour every morning.

Trying to fit in a prayer time as well as an hour walk in the morning was a real struggle, and I just didn't seem to have enough time for both. Then it dawned on me: Why couldn't I pray while I was walking? So that's what I did. I would spend an hour in the morning praying and walking. I also had a daily Bible reading schedule, so often I had verses that I was mulling over in my head as I walked.

The first few weeks of this regime, I would spend my whole "walking hour" talking to Jesus about issues, problems, needs, and ministry plans. However, one morning I got a very strong sense from God to just shut up and listen to Him. So I did. I started my walk by saying, "Okay, Lord, I'm listening, please speak to me." I just walked and waited, and God started to direct my thoughts to Him and His character. I thought about

His provision in my life, His grace and patience, His faithfulness and blessing. As I walked and meditated on Jesus, I was suddenly overwhelmed by a sense of His presence and love for me. It was at that moment that Jesus directed my thoughts to a big problem I was having at YFC, and it was as if a light was turned on in my mind. Jesus interwove His wisdom with my problem and provided an amazingly simple but brilliant solution that honored Him and reflected His character. Up until this time I had been so busy telling God about my problems that He couldn't get a word in. He just wanted me to listen. And when I did, He was able to provide the answer in the context of His character and past faithfulness.

As I spent more time with Jesus, studying and meditating on His Word and listening to Him, I started to sense His presence with me throughout the day. I would often find myself chatting to Him about things as I encountered them in my ministry and family life. In my conversations with others I would sometimes say something and realize that what I said was not consistent with how I would have normally responded, but it was a far better response that resulted in a far better outcome. The closer we get to Jesus the more He can live through us, directing our every thought, word, and action.

Worshiping Daily

What is worship? We are told in Romans, "Offer your bodies as living sacrifices, holy and pleasing to God—this is your spiritual act of worship. Do not conform any longer to the pattern of this world, but be transformed by the renewing of your mind. Then you will be able to test and approve what God's will is—his good, pleasing and perfect will."[12] In the Old Testament book of Micah we are given similar instructions:

With what shall I come before the LORD
> and bow down before the exalted God?
Shall I come before him with burnt offerings,
> with calves a year old?
Will the LORD be pleased with thousands of rams,
> with ten thousand rivers of oil?
Shall I offer my firstborn for my transgression,
> the fruit of my body for the sin of my soul?
He has showed you, O man, what is good.
> And what does the LORD require of you?
To act justly and to love mercy
> and to walk humbly with your God.[13]

Worshiping God as He requires is far more than just meeting for a short time once a week to sing choruses and hymns. Rather, it is reflecting God in our lives daily and bringing Him glory through doing His will on this earth. It involves obedience and self-sacrifice. Worship is "Walking With Jesus Daily" in such a close and intimate relationship that it transforms and renews our thinking. This allows us to know the will of God and, therefore, bring Him honor and glory daily by the way we live.

The Fruit of the Spirit

In Matthew, Jesus tells us that it is by our "fruit" that others will know whether or not we are His followers.[14] In Galatians we are given a list of spiritual fruit: "love, joy, peace, patience, kindness, goodness, faithfulness, gentleness and self-control."[15] Our spiritual fruitfulness is the ultimate test of our authenticity.

However, the only way we are going to be able to exhibit this fruit in our lives is to live by the Spirit. It is not going to come naturally, nor are we going to be able to force these things into our lives. In Ephesians 5:18 we read, "Do not get drunk on wine, which leads to debauchery. Instead, be filled with the Spirit." When you are drunk, you lose control of yourself and the alcohol takes over. Paul likens being filled with the Holy Spirit to being drunk. We need to be drunk on the Spirit, to be filled to such a degree that it is not us but the Spirit who is directing our actions and thoughts. The more we open ourselves up to Jesus by spending time with Him, the more we allow His Spirit to fill us, and the more we will be like Him.

Providing a Fertile Environment for Growing Disciples
Living in an intimate relationship with Christ empowers us to be effective disciple-makers, because it not only allows us to model discipleship to new believers, it also provides us with a much better understanding of the end product of our disciple-making process. As much as "defining" the end product is important, "knowing" the end product is a key factor in setting and achieving the target.

Clearly, making authentic disciples of Jesus requires that we have authentic disciples engaged in the disciple-making process. However, it also requires that we have communities of believers available to provide fertile ground to plant, nurture, and grow disciples—communities that are transformational in nature, authentically expressing and applying the values of the Bible and the teachings of Jesus.

As I explained at the beginning of this chapter, by profiling a disciple of Christ and using this as our point of reference for our planning in YFC, we were able to develop a more effective discipleship process. In the same way, if a local church wishes to be an effective disciple-making community it needs to move from being "program focused" to "disciple focused." This simple but challenging strategic shift will radically change the way a church operates, affecting every aspect of church governance.

Using a disciple profile as the primary measure of what is done in any church—and how it is done—will very soon move the church from a "program" approach to ministry to a "process" orientation that employs a character-based value set as the primary measurement tool. The way the church measures success will no longer be by the attendance numbers, or the amount of programs they have, or the size and quality of the buildings, or the number of staff, or how much they receive in offerings. Instead, the church will be measured by how much the members live as Jesus did. Instead of selecting a program because it looks good, or because other churches have the program, or because it will increase the attendance numbers, programs will be selected because they will help church members move closer to being true disciples of Jesus.

If there is a clear understanding that authentic discipleship has a lot to do with intimacy with Jesus, then the church will be motivated to employ processes that encourage people to spend more time with Jesus. This may result in reducing programs significantly—rather than introducing new ones—to free up people so they can spend more time with Jesus, with their families, and with those who don't yet know Jesus.

Knowing that prayer and accountability are keys to helping people become more effective in living by the values of the kingdom and motivating them to reach their families, friends, and peers, a church may choose to introduce Prayer Triplets. And the rationale for adopting the Prayer Triplet program won't be because it is the latest and greatest ministry strategy. The primary motivation for employing the program will be to help people become more engaged in prayer and to ultimately be more effective representatives of Jesus in the world.

Being confronted with the alarming rate of family breakdown in the community, and the overwhelming "busyness" of people living in the modern world, understanding that God abhors divorce,[16] and knowing the high value Jesus places on caring for children,[17] a church may choose to cease operating the many programs that gobble up people's time and separate family members. Instead, a church may replace all these programs with just one or two programs that encourage husbands and wives and families to spend more time together, and to learn to love and care for each other more.

All of these discipleship basics we've just covered can be seen as illustrations of the "deliberate strokes" a surfer takes once he or she has decided to get up to speed with the chosen wave. As the next wave of mission sweeps across the world, we are going to need a plethora of "transformational communities" ready to receive a massive harvest of the new believers. The capacity of these transformational communities to adequately care for these new believers will very much depend upon how disciple-oriented these communities are, and how many authentic disciple-makers they contain—disciple-makers who can say with Paul, "Whatever you have learned or received or heard from me, or seen in me—put it into practice."[18] The church of Jesus Christ needs to be in sync with the wave, not trying to swim after it!

NOTES

1. See Appendix: Profile of a Disciple

2. Stephen Covey, *Seven Habits of Highly Effective People* (New York: Simon & Schuster, 1989), pp. 23-24.

3. Dallas Willard, interviewed in *Leadership*, Vol. XXVI, Num. 3 (Summer 2005), p. 22.

4. Willard, p. 22.

5. Mark 2:17

6. Willard, pp. 23-24.

7. Matthew 12:34

8. Luke 6:45

9. James Dobson, *Dr. Dobson's Newsletter* (February, 2006).

10. *Zondervan NIV Bible Commentary* (Grand Rapids: Zondervan, 2002).

11. *Asbury Bible Commentary* (Grand Rapids: Zondervan, 2002).

12. Romans 12:1-2

13. Micah 6:6-8

14. Matthew 7:15-20

15. Galatians 5:22-23

16. Malachi 2:16

17. Matthew 19:13-14; Mark 9:37

18. Philippians 4:9

CHAPTER TEN

RELEASING THE POTENTIAL
OF YOUTH

In 1990 a young author named Douglas Coupland released a book titled *Generation X: Tales of an Accelerated Culture*. The book was such an accurate analysis of the youth culture of the 1990s that it quickly became a best seller. The media, social commentators, youth specialists, and popular writers were in a frenzy; finally they had a term to label the youth community of the Western world. "Generation X" was born, and Douglas Coupland became an overnight celebrity.

Of course, Douglas Coupland didn't stop writing after releasing his first best seller. Following *Generation X* he released two more books in the same genre—*Shampoo Planet*, and then, *Life After God*—each expanding on the themes and concepts introduced in *Generation X*.

Life After God is a confrontational and poignant book. In it Coupland continues to analyze and describe the postmodern youth culture, with a specific focus on young adults. He identifies the young adult community of the West as "the first generation raised without God." He deals with issues of loneliness, lack of purpose and meaning, collapse of relationships, anxiety, and apathy.

Toward the end of the book Coupland frequently refers to a
secret he wishes to share with his readers, but explains that he
is waiting for the right moment to share it. As he moves on in
his analysis of the "lostness" of the current young adult generation, he finally gets to the point where he is ready to share his
secret. The following is what he shares:

> Now—here is my secret: I tell it to you with an openness of heart
> that I doubt I shall ever achieve again, so I pray that you are in
> a quiet room as you hear these words. My secret is that I need
> God—that I am sick and can no longer make it alone. I need God
> to help me to give, because I am no longer capable of giving; to
> help me to be kind, as I no longer seem capable of kindness; to
> help me to love, as I seem beyond being able to love.[1]

Douglas Coupland, one of the most incisive and popular social commentators on the youth community of the Western
world, has arrived at the conclusion that he and his generation are emotionally, relationally, and spiritually bankrupt. And
what does he see as the answer to their desperate need? A relationship with God!

Jesus said, "Blessed are those who hunger and thirst for
righteousness, for they will be filled."[2] In *Life After God* Coupland skillfully and accurately identifies and articulates the
deep hunger and thirst of what he calls the "generation beyond
God," a generation searching for meaning and purpose—with
deep spiritual needs and hungry for the truth—but looking in all
the wrong places to have their hunger satisfied.

The Meaninglessness of Life Without God

Ecclesiastes is a book about a search for meaning. The author of Ecclesiastes—who most scholars believe to be King

Solomon—explores all that life has to offer. In chapters 1 and 2 he explains how he set out to discover what really matters in life, to discover the things that will provide ultimate satisfaction, meaning, and purpose. He tries education, entertainment, alcohol, wealth, materialism, sex, and fame. He concludes by stating, "I denied myself nothing my eyes desired; I refused my heart no pleasure. My heart took delight in all my work, and this was the reward for all my labor. Yet when I surveyed all that my hands had done and what I had toiled to achieve, everything was meaningless, a chasing after the wind; nothing was gained under the sun."[3]

The remainder of the book of Ecclesiastes is devoted to an exploration of the limitations of human wisdom and enterprise. The author ponders man's vain attempt to master his own destiny, chasing after empty dreams and ambitions that in the end are simply "meaningless, a chasing after the wind." In the final chapter of the book he comes to a conclusion:

> Remember your Creator in the days of your youth, before the days of trouble come and the years approach when you will say, "I find no pleasure in them."[4] . . . Now all has been heard; here is the conclusion of the matter: Fear God and keep his commandments, for this is the whole duty of man.[5]

The author of Ecclesiastes, after spending a lifetime exploring what is of lasting value in this world, discovers that if you want to live a productive life, if you want to find ultimate meaning and purpose, if you want your life to count for something, then get your relationship with God sorted out while you are young. Give your life over to God at the beginning of life, for nothing is worth pursuing outside of a relationship with God. Without God, life has no meaning!

The saddest thing about Ecclesiastes is that it took the author his whole life to make this discovery. It was only as he reflected on his life that he realized much of his time on the earth had been devoted to a pursuit of things, which in the end, didn't really matter. He used up his life on meaningless endeavors. He urges the readers of his book to not make the same mistake.

In Proverbs 8:36 we read, "Whoever fails to find [God's wisdom personified] harms himself." Failing to find God early in life can be enormously damaging. Young people have boundless energy and creativity that can be directed in either amazingly constructive or incredibly destructive pursuits.

Handing over your life to God in your youth provides the Creator of the universe with the opportunity to direct all your youthful energy and potential into things that matter. It provides the platform for launching a life of lasting meaning and purpose and blessing for others, a life that will have such an impact for good in the world that it will resonate throughout eternity.

The alternative is a life without God, resulting in a squandering of all that youthful energy, creativity, and potential on things that don't matter, or—even worse—on things that are incredibly destructive to the individual and to others in their circle of influence.

What Was That All About?

I have a number of key people in my life who have faithfully served and supported me as mentors and advisors. Rob is one of these mentors who walked with me through some of my most challenging leadership experiences. He was chairman of the YFC board throughout my term as National Director of YFC Australia, and was also chairman of the international board while I served as Asia Pacific Director and in my first few years as president of YFC International. He is a man whom I greatly respect for his wisdom, commitment to mission, generosity, and encouragement.

Rob started his career in building and construction in his teenage years, and right from the outset of his working life, it was clear that he was a gifted leader and entrepreneur. He very quickly established himself in his own business, and in his mid-twenties started to emerge as a major player in the construction industry. He went on to develop an international business that was hugely successful and brought him a great deal of recognition and respect from both the government and private industry.

At an early age Rob committed his life to Christ. He was active in his local church and endeavored to conduct his business according to God's principles. However, Rob shares how his primary focus was on building and managing his business. He got to a stage in his life where he looked back on about thirty years of hard work and business "success," and asked himself the question "What was that all about?" He realized—as did the author of Ecclesiastes—that without having a "God-directed" purpose to everything he did in life, it really didn't amount to much. From that point on, Rob applied all his talents, re-sources, time, and treasure to doing God's business. He has played a pivotal leadership role in a number of mission agencies and ministries worldwide, and he has definitely played a pivotal role in my life, contributing much to where I am today in my walk with Jesus.

In chapter 7 I shared the story of Gordon, another significant mentor and motivator in my life. He had a similar story to Rob's, very successful in business and at a later stage in life

realized that he really had not achieved much for the kingdom. He devoted the rest of his life to founding and growing Mobile Mission Maintenance, an organization that "serves
those who serve." Through this organization Gordon has made
a huge impact in this world by serving, encouraging, and empowering frontline missionaries, through providing resources
and support that allowed missionaries to be far more effective
and focused in their ministry.

It was largely because of Gordon's example and guidance that
Jenny and I left our careers in our early twenties and entered
into a life of mission. Using the story of his own life, Gordon
challenged us to get involved in mission while we were still
young, and to not waste a moment of our future on things that
didn't really matter.

It could be perceived that Gordon and Rob wasted the first
forty or fifty years of their lives. But our God is the great Re-
deemer. When Gordon and Rob redirected their lives to solely
serve God and grow His kingdom, God took all of their experience, wealth, and knowledge that had been accumulated over
their years in business and applied it in His service. Because of
God's grace and redemptive power, Rob and Gordon were able
to invest their past, present, and future in His service, bringing
great blessing to others and glory to God.

It is never too late to let God take charge of your life. But
it is a tragedy when people just meander through their entire
life, expending all their time, talent, and treasure investing in
their careers or businesses, accumulating material possessions,
and serving their own desires and needs. It's sad that many
never evaluate their life's direction and purpose from a kingdom perspective.

We are all going to have to give an account to our God for how we expended our lives on this earth. In Luke 12 Jesus tells a story about a businessman who invested all his time, talent, and treasure in growing his business and gaining wealth and possessions. But when this man thought he had reached a place in his life where he could finally take it easy and enjoy all his wealth, God says to him, "You fool! This very night your life will be demanded from you. Then who will get what you have prepared for yourself?" Jesus concludes this story by stating, "This is how it will be with anyone who stores up things for himself but is not rich toward God. . . . But seek his kingdom, and these things will be given to you as well. . . . Sell your possessions and give to the poor. Provide purses for yourselves that will not wear out, a treasure in heaven that will not be exhausted, where no thief comes near and no moth destroys."[6] Over and over Jesus talks about the importance of investing our lives in things that have eternal value, of allowing God's agenda to determine the priorities of our lives and the values by which we live. The alternative is a wasted life that has no lasting value.

Don't throw away your life! Make it count for God and for His kingdom. Invest all He has entrusted to you in things that have eternal value. As Mother Teresa once said, "All that is not given is lost forever."

Are You Satisfied?

Many people today are searching for satisfaction in life. This is particularly true in the church. We long to be comfortable, to find inner tranquility. The songs we sing and the messages that are delivered from the pulpit often focus on a personal relationship with Jesus that will bring satisfaction, peace, comfort, and contentment. We talk of finding "rest" in God. Yet it seems to me that the "rest" God offers has more to do with belonging, meaning, and purpose than with comfort, inner peace, and tranquility.

I think that being a healthy Christian involves a restlessness that is characterized by a general dissatisfaction with the way things are. It is this restlessness and dissatisfaction that is the catalyst for growth. If you are truly satisfied in life, then you will have no motivation to grow or to change things; but the Christian life is all about growth and change. It is about becoming more like Jesus. It is about addressing issues of injustice and need in the world. It is about calling others into a right relationship with God. It is about being dissatisfied with how things are and striving to bring more of God's kingdom values into your life and into the world.

Our attitude toward life should be similar to that of a lifeguard who is constantly alert to what is going on around him and extremely dissatisfied when others are hurting or in need. When people get caught in a "rip" in the surf and are taken out to sea, the lifeguard doesn't continue to sit on the beach sunning himself, relaxing in the warmth that God has provided. He very quickly becomes "dissatisfied" that there are people drowning in the section of the surf that he has been commissioned to patrol, and he will never be satisfied until he has dragged all of those floundering people back to the safety of the beach.

I don't want to live a satisfied, contented life. If I am dissatisfied with the way I am, then I will have the incentive to grow and become more like the person God wants me to be. If I am dissatisfied and unhappy about the fact that many young people in the world don't have a legitimate opportunity to know Jesus, then I will be motivated to work harder to give them an opportunity to be a disciple. If I am dissatisfied and disturbed by the way our egocentric, materially driven society chews up young people and spits them out with no hope and purpose in their lives, then I will fight to change the values and worldview that does this, doing all I can to bring hope and meaning to our young people.

If we are actively following Jesus, I think we should be experiencing a general discontent about the way things are, a discomfort that permeates our lives because we are Christians living in an unchristian world. The Bible doesn't picture the Christian life as being a life of ease, but one of struggle and pain, of hunger and thirst for things to be right, and an ever-present calling to be more like Jesus and share Him with the world around us.

As we make our way into this new millennium, may it be a period when the church is more and more populated with "dissatisfied" followers of Jesus. May it be an era when the church wakes up and gets involved in making a difference by effectively representing Jesus in a world that has gone horribly wrong. But even if the church as a whole continues to wallow in complacency and contentment, you can be assured that there is an emerging global community of youth who are sold out to Jesus, and who are very dissatisfied with the way things are in the world.

The next wave of mission is coming. A generation is arising that carries with it all of the energy, creativity, healthy naiveté, idealism, and hope of youth, a generation that will not rest while the world around spirals into a deeper pit of despair and lostness. They are a generation who will change the world. But to reach their full potential they need us to stand with them, to pray with them and for them, to mentor them, to encour-

age them, to equip them, to resource them, to affirm them, to
protect them, and to allow them to lead.

Nurturing to Realize the Enormous Potential of Young People
Jesus often used the example of a seed in His teaching. When
explaining the kingdom of God, He said, "It is like a mustard
seed, which is the smallest seed you plant in the ground. Yet
when planted, it grows and becomes the largest of all garden
plants, with such big branches that the birds of the air can
perch in its shade."[7]

Young believers are like seeds. They have enormous potential
stored up inside them. But just as a seed needs to be planted
in fertile ground and then watered and fed to realize its full
potential, so a young person needs to be planted in the fertile
ground of a transformational community and be nurtured and
fed to reach his or her full potential.

A generation of young believers is arising, and we in the
church have an enormous responsibility to provide the fertile
ground and the nurture and care they need to reach their full
potential. By living as authentic followers of Jesus and serving
this generation that has the potential to change the world, we
can play a vital role in the next wave of mission.

God did not call us into His kingdom to be spectators who sit
on the sidelines watching what He is doing through others. He
requires that we get involved in the affairs of the kingdom, to
invest all that He has given us in serving Him by serving others.
So get involved! Don't miss this opportunity of a lifetime.

A Horizontal View
In 1 Thessalonians we are encouraged with a glimpse of the
future:

According to the Lord's own word, we tell you that we who are still alive, who are left till the coming of the Lord, will certainly not precede those who have fallen asleep. For the Lord himself will come down from heaven, with a loud command, with the voice of the archangel and with the trumpet call of God, and the dead in Christ will rise first. After that, we who are still alive and are left will be caught up together with them in the clouds to meet the Lord in the air. And so we will be with the Lord forever. Therefore encourage each other with these words.[8]

When I am called up into the air to meet with Jesus, I want to have a "horizontal" view, not a "vertical" one. Instead of looking back at all I am leaving behind, I want to be looking around at all who are coming with me. I sincerely believe that living authentic, revolutionary lives for Jesus, and reaching, teaching, mentoring, and empowering young people to impact the world is the most strategic thing we can do to ensure as many as possible join us in that great gathering in the heavens with our Lord and Savior.

NOTES

1. Douglas Coupland, *Life After God* (New York: Pocket Books, 1994), p. 359.

2. Matthew 5:6

3. Ecclesiastes 2:10-11

4. Ecclesiastes 12:1

5. Ecclesiastes 12:13

6. Luke 12:20-21,31,33

7. Mark 4:31-32

8. 1 Thessalonians 4:16-17

APPENDIX

PROFILE OF A DISCIPLE

"Therefore go and make disciples of all nations."
Matthew 28:19

Character

- *Demonstrates a passion for God*
  - o Desires to be in God's presence, through prayer and fellowship with Him. *(Psalm 42:1; Phil 3:7-10)*
  - o Life is characterized by devotion to prayer and the Word of God. *(Josh 1:8; Psalm 1:1-3; Acts 2:42; 1 Thess 5:17)*
  - o Diligently seeks to live a life that is obedient to God's will. *(1 Sam 15:22; John 14:23; James 1:22)*
  - o Is totally dependent on God to work through them. *(Psalm 121; John 15:4-5; Acts 17:28; Phil 4:13)*
  - o Worships God with other believers in worship gatherings and through ministering together. *(Gal 5:13; Heb 10:25)*

- *Demonstrates a commitment to other young people*
  - o Disciples/mentors other young people. *(Ex 35:34; Psalm 78:5-7; Matt 28:19-20; 2 Tim 2:2)*
  - o Prays with and intercedes for young people persistently. *(Eph 1:16; 6:18; Col 4:2-4)*

- o Demonstrates an active love and support for other young people by being an advocate and motivator for godliness, evangelism, and social ministry. *(Is 58:6; Micah 6:8; 1 Tim 4:12)*
- o Acts compassionately by listening to and serving their peers. *(Mark 9:35; James 1:19)*
- o Enjoys being with other young people. *(Matt 5:13-15)*

- • *Is maturing personally*
  - o Actively pursues the mind of Christ with a kingdom perspective. *(1 Cor 2:15-16)*
  - o Demonstrates integrity, consistency, and purity. *(Psalms 22:11; 78:72; 1 Tim 2:1-2; 4:12; 6:11)*
  - o Values self-understanding and seeks to know one's gifts, personality, and emotional strengths and weaknesses. *(Psalm 139:23; Rom 12:5-13; 2 Cor 12:9-10; Eph 4:11-13, James 1:23-24)*
  - o Is committed to accountability in relation-ships. *(Eph 4:25; Gal 6:1-2; James 5:16)*
  - o Is committed to a lifelong learning and growing process with Jesus. *(Ezra 7:10; 1 Cor 9:24-27; Phil 3:12-14; Heb 6:1)*

- • *Practices biblical stewardship*
  - o Gives cheerfully, generously, and proportionately. *(Matt 6:2-4; 2 Cor 9:6-7)*
  - o Manages personal and ministry resources well. *(Matt 25:14-29; Luke 12:48)*

Family Life
- *Maintains healthy family relationships*
  - o Has a growing respect and appreciation for all family members and their roles, demonstrating appropriate submissiveness to their parent/guardian. *(Ex 20:12; Eph 6:1-3; Col 3:20)*
  - o Places a high value on family reconciliation and harmony. *(Psalm 133:1; Matt 5:9; Eph 4:3; Col 3:15)*
  - o Seeks to be an example of Christlikeness to family members. *(2 Kings 14:3; Eph 5:1-2; 1 Tim 4:12)*
  - o Pursues and encourages fellowship with God within their family context. *(Josh 24:15; Phil 2:1-2; 1 John 1:7)*

Leadership
- *Leads like Jesus*
  - o Has a servant attitude toward others. *(1 Sam 25:41; Mark 9:35; Phil 2:3-4)*
  - o Is committed to life within community. *(Col 3:12-17; 1 Peter 2:9-10; 1 John 3:16)*
  - o Inspires other "followers" by example. *(Judges 2:7; 1 Cor 11:1; 1 Tim 4:12)*

Evangelism
- *Is passionate and sensitive about evangelism*
  - o Seeks opportunities for sharing stories of faith. (*Col 4:5-6; Heb 11; 1 Peter 3:15)*
  - o Can motivate and facilitate others for mission. *(Matt 28:19-20; Rom 10:13-15; Heb 10:24)*
  - o Listens and finds appropriate local metaphors for sharing the gospel. *(Acts 17:16-34)*

- *Is aware of the world and identifies trends in today's generation*
  - o Shows compassion for the community and culture around them and listens to their peers' needs. *(Zech 7:9; Matt 25:31-46; Luke 10:25-37)*
  - o Seeks to understand trends in youth cultures, and responds appropriately. *(1 Chron 12:32; Acts 17:16-34)*
  - o Is aware of the tensions caused by the gospel within a culture. *(Matt 10:22; Luke 6:22; 1 Cor 8:1-13, Phil 2:15; Hebrews 11)*
  - o Is aware of what God is doing in and through people and events in the world. *(Psalm 46:6-11; Acts 15:2-4)*
  - o Has a heart of compassion for people at home and abroad. *(Luke 10:25-37; Acts 11:27-30; Col 3:12)*

Church Life
- *Is committed to and promotes the ministry of the local church*
  - o Is a member of a local church. *(Eph 5:30; Heb 13:17)*
  - o Actively participates in the life and ministry of his or her local church. *(Rom 12:6-8; 1 Cor 15:58)*
  - o Is involved in peer-to-peer discipleship ministry in the local church. *(Matt 28:19-20; 2 Tim 2:2)*

- *Has a kingdom mentality*
  - o Has an appreciation for the church in its varied cultural expressions. *(Acts 1:8, 15:5-20; Gal 3:28)*
  - o Is committed to the unity of God's people. *(Psalm 133:1; Matt 6:9; John 17:11; Eph 4:3-6)*

ABOUT THE AUTHOR

David Wraight and his wife, Jenny, began their ministry life in their early twenties, serving in an Aboriginal community in Western Australia, where they cared for neglected and abused Aboriginal children. Following their time in Western Australia, David served as a pastor and youth counselor at a church in Melbourne, Australia. There he developed an extensive youth ministry that included an innovative youth accommodation (housing) and counseling program. In 1990 David joined Youth for Christ, initially serving as Executive Director of YFC Melbourne, and then as National Director of YFC Australia. For five years he served as the YFC Asia Pacific Area Director, until being appointed to his current role of International President/CEO.

David and his wife have three children—Belinda, Tracey, and Michael—and currently reside in Denver, Colorado, the location of YFC International's headquarters.

ROOTED. GROUNDED.

THE DESIGN FOR DISCIPLESHIP Series

The essential Bible study series for twenty-first-century
followers of Christ.

DFD 1 Your Life in Christ
ISBN-13: 978-1-60006-004-5
ISBN-10: 1-60006-004-8

DFD 2 The Spirit-Filled Follower of Jesus
ISBN-13: 978-1-60006-005-2
ISBN-10: 1-60006-005-6

DFD 3 Walking with Christ
ISBN-13: 978-1-60006-006-9
ISBN-10: 1-60006-006-4

DFD 4 The Character of a Follower of Jesus
ISBN-13: 978-1-60006-007-6
ISBN-10: 1-60006-007-2

DFD 5 Foundations for Faith
ISBN-13: 978-1-60006-008-3
ISBN-10: 1-60006-008-0

DFD 6 Growing in Discipleship
ISBN-13: 978-1-60006-009-0
ISBN-10: 1-60006-009-9

DFD 7 Our Hope in Christ
ISBN-13: 978-1-60006-010-6
ISBN-10: 1-60006-010-2

DFD Leader's Guide
ISBN-13: 978-1-60006-011-3
ISBN-10: 1-60006-011-0

To order copies, visit your local Christian bookstore, call NavPress at
1-800-366-7788, or log on to www.navpress.com.
To locate a Christian bookstore near you, call 1-800-991-7747.

AN UNCOMMON DEVOTIONAL FOR TODAY'S STUDENT.

The Message//REMIX Solo

Eugene Peterson
ISBN-13: 978-1-60006-105-9
ISBN-10: 1-60006-105-2

Transform your quiet time.

This innovative devotional is designed to change how you interact with God's Word. *The Message//REMIX: Solo* revolves around *lectio divina*, or "divine reading," an ancient approach to exploring Scripture updated for today's students. Each devotion delivers a unique, contemplative study that will encourage you to: Read, Think, Pray, Live.

So don't just read the Bible. Get engaged with God's Word and let it revolutionize your life.

To order copies, visit your local Christian bookstore, call NavPress at 1-800-366-7788, or log on to www.navpress.com.
To locate a Christian bookstore near you, call 1-800-991-7747.

THE HIGH SCHOOL SURVIVAL GUIDE
Making the Most of the Best Time of Your Life (So Far)

Adam Palmer
ISBN-13: 978-1-60006-129-5
ISBN-10: 1-60006-129-X

High school is the ultimate learning experience.

Popular author Adam Palmer takes a laugh-out-loud look at life before adulthood. With his hip and humorous style, Adam shares both personal and collected wisdom about the high school experience. From grade expectations to the opposite sex to balancing the studies with the social, Adam prepares students of any age for a four years they'll never forget.

To order copies, visit your local Christian bookstore, call NavPress at
1-800-366-7788, or log on to www.navpress.com.
To locate a Christian bookstore near you, call 1-800-991-7747.

EMBRACE THE CHARACTER OF GOD

Walking with God Bible Studies

A new study series that explores our endless God.

Our Faithful Friend

ISBN-13: 978-1-57683-620-0
ISBN-10: 1-57683-620-7

God longs for an intimate relationship with each of us. But what does it mean to be friends with the Lord? This study highlights a God who can always be trusted and who is forever faithful.

Our Loving Father

ISBN-13: 978-1-60006-219-3
ISBN-10: 1-60006-219-9

God's love is infinite in measure. No one loves more deeply or forgives more readily. This insightful study explores God's endless love and encourages readers to model His perfect example.

Our Powerful Helper

ISBN-13: 978-1-57683-627-9
ISBN-10: 1-57683-627-4

God's power is made perfect in our weakness. This study shows readers that He can be trusted in all circumstances and that His wondrous power is made available to us through prayer.

Our Wise Counselor

ISBN-13: 978-1-60006-220-9
ISBN-10: 1-60006-220-2

God delights to give wisdom to those who passionately seek it. This study encourages readers to not only pursue this gift but also apply God's higher wisdom in every area of their lives.

To order copies, visit your local Christian bookstore, call NavPress at 1-800-366-7788, or log on to www.navpress.com.
To locate a Christian bookstore near you, call 1-800-991-7747.